WITH SO-EAY-635

# Investigative Reporting

# Investigative Reporting

## by Marilyn Moorcroft

FRANKLIN WATTS
New York/London/Toronto/Sydney
1981

Library of Congress Cataloging in Publication Data

Moorcroft, Marilyn.
    Investigative reporting.

    Bibliography: p.
    Includes index.
    SUMMARY: Discusses aspects of investigative
journalism, including some of the legalities involved
in the pursuit of truth in reporting.
    1. Reporters and reporting—Juvenile literature.
[1. Reporters and reporting]     I. Title.
PN4781.M59            070.4'3            80-25586
ISBN 0-531-02871-2

I wish to thank the following people for their advice, help, criticism, and/or moral support at various stages in the conception, researching, organization, writing, and editing of this book: Professor John D. Mitchell, Chairman, Newspaper Division, S. I. Newhouse School of Public Communications, Syracuse University; Ed Schneider; Marvin Siegel; Frank Leary; Jim O'Hanlon; Ellen Frankfort; Verne Moberg; William E. Burrows, Associate Professor, Department of Journalism, New York University; and Maury Solomon, my clear-thinking and patient editor. The following people and organizations, whose addresses are listed in the Appendix, were generous in providing me with literature and copies of their publications: Howard Bray, Executive Director, the Fund for Investigative Journalism, Inc.; Alan Reitman, Associate Director, American Civil Liberties Union; the Reporters Committee for Freedom of the Press; and Amnesty International.

I would also like to thank the British Information Service, the staff of the Jefferson Market Branch of the New York Public Library, my brother J. Ronald Moorcroft, Frank Nastasi, and George and Pamela Ballou for their help.

# Contents

TO MY MOTHER,
EMMA D. MOORCROFT,
WITH LOVE

Two persons may contradict each other
and both speak truth,
for the truth of one person may be
opposite the truth of another.

John Horne Tooke,
The Diversions of Purley
(London, 1829)


Yet, the first bringing of unwelcome news
has but a losing office,
and his tongue sounds ever after
as a sullen bell.

William Shakespeare,
*Henry IV*, Part 2
(a favorite quotation of
Katharine Graham,
publisher, *Washington Post*)

The function of news is to
signalize an event;
the function of truth is to
bring to light the hidden facts,
to set them into relation
with each other, and make
a picture of reality on which
men can act.

Walter Lippmann


Actions were taken that
we called containment—
and the press called cover-up—
and the courts called
conspiracy to obstruct justice.

H. R. Haldeman,
*The Ends of Power*

# Chapter 1.
# The Gadfly
# That Protects Us All

The Book of Esther in the Bible describes one of the earliest known cases of investigative reporting. The familiar elements are all there: corrupt plotting by Haman, a high-placed government official; uncovering of the plot by Mordecai, who reports it to his niece, the queen; and Esther placing her life in danger by investigating the plot and reporting it to the king and her scrupulous concern for the truth as well as cleverness in getting Haman to incriminate himself.

Shakespeare sets up a similar scenario in *Hamlet*. Again, all the elements are present: a corrupt king and his complacent administration; the exposure of the plot by the Ghost (in a sense, a leak[1] from the hereafter); a careful investigation of the facts by Hamlet; and an eventual verification of the evidence in the queen's and Laertes' confessions condemning the king.

Esther and Hamlet, however, were not investigative reporters. They were the main characters in their respective

---

[1] For the definition of this and other journalistic and legal terms, see the glossary at the back of this book.

dramas, very much affected by the outcome of their own investigations and highly subjective in their attitudes toward the other characters.

Investigative reporting is only one of several kinds of journalism. But it is the best known and most highly respected variety. When reporters Carl Bernstein and Bob Woodward wrote front-page stories in the *Washington Post* that gave impetus to the Watergate investigation, which in turn ultimately led to the resignation of President Richard M. Nixon, we were all suddenly awed by the visible power of the press. We were impressed that in a system as complex, monolithic, sprawling, and bureaucratic as ours, two relatively unknown persons such as Woodward and Bernstein could have such a significant impact.

The Watergate period was an emotional time in American history, unprecedented in that it led to the resignation of a president. Two young writers, one a college dropout, tackled a presidential administration and helped bring it down against all odds. The story of their actions so captured the public's imagination that it was turned into a best-selling book and successful film called *All the President's Men.*

However, the two reporters did not, strictly speaking, investigate anything at all. They reported information that was made available to them by people inside the institution they were questioning. The investigations that actually resulted in the president's resignation were conducted by the institution itself.

Woodward and Bernstein benefited from having a number of trustworthy sources, from a willingness to check and recheck information, and from the fact that their employer, the *Washington Post,* had a political leaning that made it prepared to back an antiadministration exposé. The reporters were skeptical. They were willing to probe. But they did not perform a true investigation themselves.

Investigative reporters are not arms of the law. They cannot compel testimony, summon witnesses, undertake elaborate scientific inquiries to verify data, or develop expert evidence. It is the courts and their executive arms, the police, that have the power to gather and interpret evidence—to investigate. Congress can investigate also.

In 1963 a reporter known to the author and who was acquainted with the facts concerning movements of the U.S. Second Fleet during the Bay of Pigs invasion, decided to write the story of those movements. He was angered at the statements of the Kennedy administration that the navy had not been involved in the attempted invasion.

The reporter submitted his article to a then-prominent but now extinct national magazine, which referred it directly to the navy for verification. Since the navy for over a year had been trying to keep a lid of secrecy on the movements of the Second Fleet during the Bay of Pigs invasion, navy public affairs officers denied every line of the story. (This, despite the fact that a well-known naval officer had apparently already verified some elements of the story when describing his own actions during that period.) The magazine editor asked the reporter to reveal the names of others who could verify his story. The reporter declared that he could not do so without endangering his sources, some of whom were still under naval jurisdiction. Pressured by the navy, one of whose officers was in fact present at the conference between the editor and the reporter, the magazine refused to publish the article.

What happened afterward illustrates a common reaction of officialdom to a threat of exposure. A cover was put on the reporter's mail. A tap was placed on his telephone. His associates in and out of the navy were harassed, threatened, and interrogated. At least one person in the navy was subsequently dismissed on trumped-up charges. Professional associates were approached and questioned. It was not until the reporter made it clear that he did not intend to resubmit his article that the harassment stopped.

Actions of this kind are always unofficial of course, to say nothing of illegal. No government official admits to them. But even without such illegal or unauthorized behavior, investigative reporters still must contend with obstacles that are officially and legally placed in their paths.

More than one hundred subpoenas a year—for notes,

tapes, photographs, and sources—have been issued in recent years to reporters across the United States. The magazine *The News Media and the Law,* published by the Reporters Committee for Freedom of the Press, reports many cases nationwide in which newspeople are ordered to disclose their sources, barred from courtrooms or hearing rooms, or prevented from seeing court records that a judge has ordered sealed, often on the uncontested motion of one attorney.

On May 31, 1978, the Supreme Court handed down a decision that may be having a chilling effect on investigative reporting. The Court reversed a lower court's decision, saying that police, armed with search warrants, may legally search a newspaper office if they have reasonable cause to believe they will find evidence that can be used in a criminal proceeding.

The original case arose in 1971 when police searched a campus newspaper, the *Stanford Daily.* The police were looking for unspecified material that would help them identify suspects involved in a demonstration in which some officers had been injured. The newspaper protested the issuance of the warrant on the grounds that there was no reasonable cause to suspect that anyone working for the newspaper had been involved in the riot and that the paper's notes, photographs, and other materials generated while covering the riot were privileged.

Traditionally a reporter's notes are, in fact, privileged. Though the lower court ruled for the newspaper, on appeal the Supreme Court reversed the decision. Whether this ruling will induce the press to now censor itself remains to be seen.

That power corrupts is a truism. That leaders in government, business, labor, education, and even sports and the arts sometimes use their positions to seek personal gain or bestow privilege is also well known. Certainly the temptation to seek profits is always at least as great as the opportunity to do so. Even the Boy Scouts of America, in 1974, was not above lying about its membership figures so as to qualify for federal aid.[2]

---

[2] David Anderson and Peter Benjaminson, *Investigative Reporting* (Bloomington, Ind.: Indiana University Press, 1976), p. 17.

The role of the press in uncovering governmental improprieties is a primary one. The exposure of corruption is central to the duties of investigative reporters. Secrecy is the adversary, especially in government but also in business and other spheres of the private sector. Osborn Elliott has worked for both *Newsweek* and the city of New York. He has had the advantage of seeing government from the outside, as a reporter, and from the inside, as a deputy mayor. He writes:

> *Years ago, a* Newsweek *colleague left to enter public service; after a while, I asked him, from his new vantage point, how much he figured he had known about any given story when he was a working journalist. "About 15 percent," was his rather insulting reply. I would put the percentage higher, but still far below what most journalists think it to be.*[3]

Some secrecy might be justified, since few can work effectively in a goldfish bowl. Still, reporters are mandated by the nature of their jobs to "get the story." And penetrating such secrecy requires every possible tactic in the craft of journalism—the craft of reporting daily events.

The word *journalism* comes to us from the Latin *diurnalis* ("daily") through French, in which language *jour* means "day." *Journal,* in one definition, still means a daily record, an account of day-to-day events. Possibly the first "newspaper" of which we have any knowledge was the *Acta Diurna* ("Daily Acts"). It was published in ancient Rome and provided news of both official and social events (court news, decrees, birth notices, marriage announcements, and so forth). It was posted on a public board and took the place of the modern newspaper. The minutes of the senate proceedings, or *Acta Senatus,* were also issued but usually kept in an archive, where special permission was needed to look at them.

The *Acta* were the archetype of what we might call ruminative journalism—the publication of information that

3 Osborn Elliott, "From City Desk to City Hall: The Odyssey of an Erstwhile Journalist," *The New York Times Magazine,* August 28, 1977, p. 31.

has been swallowed whole from another source and then, in the manner of a ruminant beast, regurgitated. The modern trade term for this is stenographic journalism, as if a stenographer had taken it down in shorthand and added or changed nothing.[4] The only journalistic skill required for this type of reporting, other than an ability to write, is the ability to mask the fact that what is being written is merely a paraphrase of a handout.

In some instances, official publications are of great value. The *Federal Register,* the *Congressional Record,* various state registers, numerous commercial registers, and a host of trade papers provide the information necessary to the conduct of business and government. And as long as readers know that what they are reading is an official handout, no harm is done.

The essayist, practicing what we might call contemplative journalism, is another of modern journalism's ancestors. Since Montaigne (whose *Essays* are among the finest ever written) in the sixteenth century and Joseph Addison and Richard Steele, who published the famous journals, the *Tatler* and the *Spectator,* in the early eighteenth century, the essay has been an honorable part of reporting.

Essays are usually written from an existing body of knowledge possessed by the writer. It is rare indeed that the essay, in the conventional sense, reflects new investigation. Yet the skills of the essayist are necessary to the investigative reporter, whose talent must include an ability to handle a logical flow of thought and to show important points in relation to each other. Also like the essayist, an investigative reporter benefits from a broad understanding in many different fields of knowledge.

Argumentative, or adversary, journalism, runs counter to accepted contemporary opinion, and the alternative media are its usual channels of expression. Thus, at various times in the history of the United States, the causes of abolition (anti-slavery), feminism, socialism, unionism, Prohibitionism (for-

---

[4] Edward J. Epstein, *Between Fact and Fiction: The Problem of Journalism* (New York: Random House, 1975), p. 4.

bidding the sale of alcoholic beverages), repeal of the Prohibition Amendment, the Vietnam antiwar movement, and equal rights for homosexuals have all reached an audience through the alternative media.

Argumentative journalism does not answer to the ordinary rules covering objective reporting. One expects it to omit facts and to use the forensic techniques of argument and debate to destroy opposing arguments. One can enjoy such techniques in editorials, in pamphlets and tracts, and in the columns of political essayists such as Max Lerner and William Buckley. But adversary tactics—argumentative journalism— weaken factual reporting.

Descriptive journalism is the true mainstream of the craft, which at its best describes reality (so far as "reality" can be determined) as it is—objectively, fairly, and accurately. The investigative journalist, however, does not merely describe surface reality nor rewrite official handouts, but probes carefully beneath to determine the relevant truths affecting the people—the public. Investigative reporting is the backbone of the free press in the modern world.

Although not part of the government, the press is essential to the health and well-being of the body politic. Its importance was abundantly clear to the men who framed the Constitution; Jefferson even suggested that a free press was more important than a formal system of public education.

The English historian Thomas Macaulay coined the term "fourth estate" to describe the unique role of the press. In nineteenth-century England the "three estates" referred to the three ruling branches of the British government. In an 1828 essay, Macaulay wrote, "The gallery in which the reporters sit has become a fourth estate of the realm"—so powerful a force had the press become in English politics.

In the United States today, the press remains an important check on political power and its abuses. At its best, the press prods, pokes, questions, exposes, and serves as a gadfly to remind those in high public office that their actions are being monitored for the sake of the people being governed. If they do their job well, investigative journalists report facts and describe realities as objectively and fairly as possible. But if they fail to probe below the level of the obvious, their work may hardly be distinguishable from stenographic journalism. On the other hand, if they fail in objectivity and fairness, their work becomes biased and suspect.

Muckraking reporters of the late nineteenth and early twentieth centuries, such as Lincoln Steffens, Ida Tarbell, and Upton Sinclair, tended to be solo stars. Today's investigative reporters, for the most part, are inclined to be somewhat less flamboyant—and more institutionalized.

In 1969 the Fund for Investigative Journalism was founded to promote and financially support the often expensive and lengthy investigations by reporters. In 1970 the Reporters Committee for Freedom of the Press was founded, to protect and shield investigative reporters and to fight for First Amendment rights wherever necessary. And each year, one of the Pulitzer Prizes is awarded specifically for investigative reporting.

The art of investigative reporting is a relatively new one. Reporters entering the profession of journalism after World War II almost invariably chose one of two main directions. They became reporters (by definition investigative, particularly into possible corruption) and moved from there to rewrite desks in the newsroom. Or they became special-feature editors or columnists.

Journalists who lacked the drive of the reporter, who liked writing but disliked probing, gravitated toward the special features and columns. Reporters, on the other hand, were often probers without a talent for writing, a talent that might or might not develop with time.

Even after graduating to the rewrite desk, these journalists were still reporters, since a major task of the rewrite person was to direct the on-site beat reporter, often younger and less experienced, as to what questions to ask, of whom to ask them, and so forth.

Two later developments ultimately made it necessary to designate investigative journalism as a particular category with distinctive characteristics of its own. The first of these

8

developments concerned a rise in the level of sophistication in the area of public relations and publicity. Since the time of Joseph Goebbels (Adolf Hitler's propaganda minister), government, business, the arts, and other institutions have all come to realize the potential for shaping public opinion in order to win support for their cause. And they do not hesitate to avail themselves of the means for doing so.

Neil Sheehan, who with other reporters wrote *The New York Times* articles based on the Pentagon Papers (an official government report that traced the history of U.S. decision-making in regard to Vietnam), said in his introduction to the paperback edition:

> *The segments of the public world—Congress, the news media, the citizenry, even international opinion as a whole—are regarded from within the world of the government insider as elements to be influenced. The policy memorandums [in the Pentagon Papers] repeatedly discuss ways to move these outside "audiences" in the desired direction, through such techniques as the controlled release of information and appeals to patriotic stereotypes. . . .*[5]

The publicist's craft, at its most sophisticated, is to select from the information available about the client or employer those facts that show the client in a favorable light and which are of greatest interest to the public. At its basest level, it is to put out lies and half-truths and hope to have them accepted as facts.

Especially in the realms of business and finance and science and technology, the reporter often lacks the specific knowledge to make independent judgments about news developments. It becomes necessary therefore to rely to some degree on news sources who are also, unfortunately, public relations practitioners. In government, publicists or news sec-

---

[5] *The Pentagon Papers,* as published by *The New York Times;* based on investigative reporting by Neil Sheehan; written by Neil Sheehan *et al.* (New York: Bantam, 1971), p. xiii.

retaries are frequently as close as the reporter can get to the newsmakers themselves. Sometimes, if the publicist is very skillful, a reporter might fall into the lazy habit of merely accepting and refining—in glorified stenographic fashion—the information handed out.

However, most investigative journalists are not fooled by publicists. As coauthors David Anderson and Peter Benjaminson write, "investigative reporters share a certain abiding faith in human nature: a faith that someone, somehow, is working against the public interest." [6] The investigative journalist questions everything—public statements made in press conferences, the contents of press releases, information from public sources, everything. He or she takes the information given, puts it together with other known facts on the subject and, if the pieces fail to fit, gathers information from additional sources. A calm persistence that chips away at the veneer of reality in order to discover the underlying truth is the most effective approach. Persistence, patience, intelligence, a broad understanding of the subject at hand, more persistence, and courage—plus a knack for organizing piles of small bits of information into a larger, more accurate, and more comprehensive picture—these are the ideal attributes of the investigative reporter, especially in penetrating those barriers erected by publicists.

The second development leading to a specific need for investigative journalism was the rise of television journalism.

Television reporters are in most cases not reporters at all. They are (and are referred to as) "talent"—front-of-camera personalities, selected for being photogenic, amiable, and attractive, but not necessarily penetrating or smart. Exceptions, such as Walter Cronkite, who *are* true reporters, are often carry-overs from radio reporting—which retains some of the characteristics of true journalism—or newspaper reporting. Most television news personalities do actually do reporting, that is, they do not actually ferret out the facts, although some interview newsmakers.

[6] Anderson and Benjaminson, *Investigative Reporting,* pp. 3–4.

Besides being limited by its need for reporters with suitable TV personalities, television is straitjacketed by its format. It is time-limited as no newspaper is ever space-limited. The more time devoted in a broadcast to one story, the less time that can be given to another because all must fit into the same, say, twenty-four-minute span. A newspaper, on the other hand, can expand its coverage—in theory, at least—virtually without limit, because it exists in space, not in time. Slim newspapers are that way not because the news is sparse but because advertising is. And a newspaper fat with ads hungers for news to prevent its pages from appearing overly commercial or lacking in redeeming social value.

Since reporting on television rapidly turned into a show-business exercise of headline reading, it became necessary to distinguish true reporting as a thing apart. Hence, the growth of the specific art of investigative journalism.

Investigative reporters who do appear on television are often not camera personalities. They may indeed be awkward on camera, are probably not photogenic, and will not generally have been trained in the use of body and voice as are the regular news personalities. But they possess the ability to wait patiently while a story develops, to probe skillfully, to assemble small bits of information into a meaningful picture, and to relate a story intelligently.

Investigative reporting was thus in part a reaction to the smooth, bland, dealer-in-headlines conventional television news personality. Simultaneously, it was also a reaction to the growth of the descriptive journalism that relies on the handouts of publicists and public relations people.

Journalism is sometimes considered to be superficial in thought, popular in slant, and hurried in composition. Investigative journalism, as it has developed, may be popular in slant, but it is not generally superficial or hurried. Investigation, as defined by the dictionary, is "a systematic, minute, and thorough attempt to learn the facts about something complex or hidden." Investigative reporters, in their attempt to learn the facts, ask searching questions. They examine public records. They question public figures and public employees at

11

all levels. They make telephone inquiries by the hundreds. Information leaked to them is checked over and over again. They work through a network of trusted contacts, carefully built up over time.

An investigative report may take days, weeks, even months to complete. Six-month investigations are commonplace. And the results can be highly gratifying, as when a sinister plot to victimize the public, or specific targets such as the elderly or children, is exposed.

Because of the kinds of results achieved, investigative journalists are an honored and respected group. Of course, more people claim the title than deserve it. But the true investigative reporter can always be recognized by his or her work, which is characterized by objectivity, fairness, thoroughness, accuracy, careful attention to detail, and the rare courage that places a higher value on uncovering truth than on personal safety.

Thus, it is important that investigative reporters generally not play an adversary role or participate in the luxury of partisanship; to do either would make their work suspect.

Investigative reporters rely heavily on sources whose identity is necessarily kept confidential. It takes courage to protect one's sources, especially in view of the fact that the First Amendment, which guarantees freedom of the press, does not, in light of the 1978 Supreme Court decision, grant to reporters any freedom from search or seizure by warrant-armed police. Nor does the Constitution protect reporters from disclosure of sources under oath, except for the limited protection provided by state shield laws and those Supreme Court rulings that clearly support a balance between a free press and fair trials.

Obviously, freedom of the press is meaningless without the equivalent freedom to gather and process information without interference. In the past investigative and other reporters have frequently put their own freedoms on the line in confronting the power of government and have sometimes suffered for their determination to assert those freedoms and to fulfill their responsibilities to the public. That they continue to do so puts us all in their debt, for their work is essential to the public good. Democratic institutions cannot survive without an informed public, and it is the investigative journalist who is today chiefly responsible for keeping people informed.

# Chapter 2.
# A Historical
# Perspective

Messengers and town criers were the first bearers of news. They would cry out their messages as they walked up and down the streets, or they would stand in public gathering places and read their proclamations aloud. Later, news was written and disseminated by professional letter writers. It was also circulated in taverns and written up in gossipy broadside ballads for those few who could read and write.

Printing was invented in China, movable type was first used in Korea, but the West credits Johann Gutenberg as the first to invent movable type in Europe, around 1454. The poor German had to sell his press to pay off his debts, but for civilization his invention was priceless. Printing flourished in the late fifteenth century, although newspapers weren't to appear for another century and a half.

The first English newspaper, Nathaniel Butter's *Weekly Newes,* was published in 1622. The first paper to publish regularly was the *London Gazette,* in 1665.

A landmark in the history of freedom of the press occurred in England about this time. When poet John Milton and his wife separated soon after their marriage in 1643,

Milton thought divorce a logical solution. He wrote several "tracts" on divorce and, charged with heresy, was ordered to appear in court to defend himself. But Milton felt he had the right to print whatever he wanted. So he wrote another piece in 1644, strongly defending freedom of the Press. Bearing the long Latin name *Areopagitica,* the essay reads, in part:

> *For this is not the liberty which we can hope, that no grievance ever should arise in the Commonwealth, that let no man in this world expect; but when complaints are freely heard, deeply considered, and speedily reformed, then is the utmost bound of civil liberty attained that wise men look for.*[7]

And so begins our own tradition of freedom of the press.

Daniel Defoe, author of the novel *Robinson Crusoe,* is usually recognized as the father of modern journalism. His pamphlet *The Shortest Way with Dissenters* and its anti-Tory views led him the shortest way to jail. From 1704 to 1713 he published his influential *Review.* The life of this magazine paralleled the growth in political power of the English press. In the *Journal of the Plague Years,* Defoe gave clear, objective, comprehensive, and concise coverage of the London plague and fire.

Issues of the *London Gazette* crossed the Atlantic and inspired American printers to print their own native newspapers. The first paper in America was *Publick Occurrences, Both Forreign and Domestick,* published in Boston in 1690. It was banned shortly after the first issue came to the attention of the Massachusetts governor and council, who charged Benjamin Harris, the paper's publisher, with failure to obtain a license. (One had to have a license in those days to publish newspapers. Today one needs a license only to broadcast.)

The *Boston Gazette,* founded in 1719, published news

[7] Quoted by *The* I. F. Stone's Weekly *Reader,* ed. Neil Middleton (New York: Vintage Books, 1973), p. ix.

for the patriots during the Revolution. Benjamin Franklin's brother James was its first printer. In the early 1720s, James Franklin began printing the *New-England Courant,* which had a lifespan of five years. The closest thing to investigative journalism yet, the *Courant* vowed to "expose the Vices and Follies of Persons of all Ranks and Degrees"—to be sure, "under fein'd Names." [8] Its favorite target was Cotton Mather and his Puritan brethren. Ben, in 1722, added his own spicy column, the "Dogood Papers," which had as its target people and issues of old Boston. James dared to criticize even the governor and as a result was thrown into jail.

The *Boston News-Letter,* the first American paper to publish regularly, came out in 1704 and died a Royalist paper during the Revolution. It was "published by Authority," meaning that each issue needed to have the governor's prior approval. (Prior restraint, or censorship, is now prohibited by the First Amendment.) None of the articles in this paper was investigative. Rather, the contents were mainly informative, telling of ship arrivals, Indian attacks, fires, and sermons. Once there was a firsthand report on the death of Bluebeard the pirate. In the beginning, newspapers were nothing but the tools of government, business, and other special interests.

Because printers could run off papers in large numbers and distribute them to a lot of people, the government feared losing the upper hand. So it passed a series of libel laws. Libel refers to defamation in print; what is written may or may not be true. Libel laws had the positive effect of offsetting the frequent character assassinations in the press in those days.

John Peter Zenger was an early American printer involved in a famous libel trial. The *New York Weekly Journal,* a popular party paper in the 1730s, was published by Zenger, a man whose name has become synonymous with a free press. Week after week the *Journal* waged verbal war on the *New York Gazette,* the paper of the "court" party of Governor William Cosby. Zenger implied that the government of Cosby

[8] Quoted by Frank Luther Mott in *American Journalism: A History: 1690–1960* (New York: Macmillan, 1968), p. 18.

was dealing arbitrarily and recklessly with the rights and property of the people. He and his friends also wrote on the concepts of liberty and representative government, essentially new ideas drawn from the writings of Cato, Swift, and Addison. Charges of libel were made against Zenger, but twice the grand jury refused to indict him. Governor Cosby grew furious, and his council had Zenger arrested for vilifying the governor's administration. Refused bail, Zenger was forced to stay in jail for nine months, but he still published indirectly by "Speaking to my servants thru' the Hole of the Door of the Prison." [9]

Lawyers agreeing to defend Zenger were harassed or even disbarred. Then, when his trial was due to begin, a prominent eighty-year-old lawyer named Andrew Hamilton, at the request of Zenger's friends, came up from Philadelphia to defend Zenger.

Hamilton argued that if an alleged libel could be proven true, it should be admitted as evidence, a new concept in jurisprudence, and that the jury had the right to determine what constituted a libel. In his appeal to the jury, Hamilton denounced arbitrary power:

> *Power may justly be compared to a great river which, while kept within its due bounds is both beautiful and useful; but when it overflows its banks, it is then too impetuous to be stemmed, it bears down all before it and brings destruction. . . .* [10]

He also supported the right of the governed to speak out freely against excessive power:

> *It is not the cause of the poor printer [Zenger], nor of New York, alone; No! It may . . . affect every freeman that lives under a British government on*

[9] Quoted by Mott, *American Journalism*, p. 34.

[10] Ibid., p. 36.

*the main of America. It is the best cause. It is the cause of liberty . . . the liberty both of exposing and opposing arbitrary power by speaking and writing Truth.*[11]

The jury pronounced Zenger not guilty, and the verdict in the colony of New York echoed up and down the coast. Although it took many years for the freedoms and legal principles Hamilton spoke of to become law, the trial was politically important. It made people far more aware of the issue of individual rights, especially the right to a free press. And, forty-one years later, the colonists would declare their independence from England.

Very much at home in the turmoil of pre-Revolutionary days was a journalist whose favorite occupation was writing essays and pamphlets. Thomas Paine, a propagandist, wrote for the *Pennsylvania Magazine,* the last issue of which contained the Declaration of Independence. Paine was also the author of the rousing tract *Common Sense,* published in January 1776 and circulated throughout the colonies to tip the scales in favor of independence from England. Over 120,000 copies of *Common Sense* were printed and distributed.

Although it was true that the British misuse of power had been assailed by several American newspapers for a long while and that a free press and free speech had been supported by Americans before Thomas Paine, *Common Sense* came out just at the peak of the dissent and thereby played a major role in moving America toward liberty and eventually toward adopting the Bill of Rights as part of the Constitution.[12]

In the early nineteenth century, journalism was linked to the growth of political parties. A newspaper often served as the voice of a party. Horace Greeley got his start publishing two campaign papers, the *Jeffersonian* and the *Log Cabin.*

---

[11] Ibid., p. 37.

[12] See the appendix for all amendments to the Constitution relevant to the subject of this book.

Inventions such as the rotary press, in mid-century, and the Mergenthaler Linotype machine, late in the century, led to mass circulation. Newspapers were truly becoming a democratic institution—papers for the people. And it was businessmen who were primarily responsible for this democratization of the news.

In fact, journalism during this time was dominated by three leading journalist-publishers: Horace Greeley, Joseph Pulitzer, and William Randolph Hearst. Their lives span one hundred and forty years of American journalism, from Greeley's birth in 1811 to Hearst's death in 1951.

Greeley, at age thirty, founded the *New York Tribune,* a penny daily (one of the first) with Whig leanings. It was not sensational, like other cheap papers. Rather, it was tasteful, even literary. Its editorials were intelligent and influential.

The *Tribune* soon became a strong voice for social reform. For example Greeley, a Socialist, was a leader in the antislavery movement. His editorials reflected his views and became a model for modern newspaper editorials.

The nationally distributed *Weekly Tribune* grew to have an unprecedented circulation of 200,000, and it made Horace Greeley's name a household word across the land. Greeley advised his poorer readers to start new lives in the country. "Go West, young man, go West," was his familiar advice. On Greeley's staff, and brilliant in their own right, were feminist and transcendentalist Margaret Fuller and Socialist Charles Dana, the managing editor who later would purchase the *New York Sun.*

The interview, that all-important tool in American journalism, was pioneered by James Gordon Bennett of the *New York Herald.* Horace Greeley, too, interviewed people, among them Brigham Young, the great Mormon religious leader. Some critics called interviewing an invasion of privacy. Satirized in cartoons, the prying reporter with flippant questions at first was met only with contempt. A technique in journalism that could be used for good or ill, interviewing later developed into a fine craft.

Greeley was the first president of the New York Printers'

Union, now Typographical Union No. 6—the same union that struck the New York papers in 1963. Greeley, the social reformer, would be remembered most for his desire to uplift the masses and for his influence on the modern editorial page.

Joseph Pulitzer, a cultured man of Jewish-German-Hungarian descent, arrived in St. Louis, Missouri, penniless. He eventually bought two newspapers there, the *Post* and the *Dispatch,* combined them, and started the *St. Louis Post-Dispatch* on its road to success. Later he went to New York and bought out the declining *World* from railroad mogul Jay Gould. Emphasizing human interest news, he initiated a whole new trend in journalism.

The *World* was a paper of crusades and causes—in short, of advocacy journalism. It exposed the Bell Telephone monopoly, improved the treatment of immigrants on Ellis Island, and raised money to build a pedestal for the Statue of Liberty. (Modern investigative journalism, in contrast, attempts a more objective approach, with no aim in mind except that of revealing to the public all the facts concerning a situation or an event.) *World* reporters, male and female, scoured New York, looking for interesting stories. One reporter, Elizabeth Cochran, feigned insanity at Blackwell's Island asylum in order to expose conditions there. Also known as Nelly Bly, the *World's* "stunt" reporter, Cochran beat the 80-days-around-the-world record of Jules Verne's fictional hero, completing the trip in 72 days and 6 hours.

Of course, newspaper crusades were not exclusively the province of the *World*. A landmark crusade of this period (1870–71) was waged by *The New York Times,* along with *Harper's Weekly,* against Tammany Hall—a group of New York politicians headed by "Boss" William M. Tweed. Tammany robbed the city of New York of $200 million—by paying huge salaries and handing out many lucrative contracts. Much of the money, of course, went to Tammany as kickbacks. One plasterer, the *Times* reported, was paid $50,000 a day for his work on a courthouse then under construction, a building that today houses New York's Municipal Archives.

20

John Foord of the *Times* did an in-depth study of the city's finances to prove corruption, and Louis J. Jenning wrote editorials that denounced Boss Tweed and his Ring. George Jones, publisher of the *Times,* refused a bribe of $5 million not to publish the city records the *Times* had acquired. And Thomas Nast, whose satirical cartoons for *Harper's Weekly* were likewise instrumental in ridding the city of the corrupt Ring, also refused a bribe—in the form of an offer to send him to Europe to study art! The publication by the *Times* of the incriminating evidence resulted in the prosecution of Ring members. They subsequently lost at the polls.

It was Joseph Pulitzer's policies and crusades, however, that led to what was known as the New Journalism (not to be confused with the New Journalism of the 1960s). Besides crusades, sensationalism, and personal gossip, the *World* included excellent coverage of serious news; sober, liberal editorials; illustrations, photos, and political cartoons; and promotional gimmicks, such as coupons and contests. When Pulitzer died, he left money to start Columbia University's School of Journalism, which in 1917 began awarding the Pulitzer Prizes.

William Randolph Hearst was a publisher whose name and paper, the *Journal,* became one with yellow journalism— a lurid, sensational type of reporting whose modern counterpart is the tabloid. Government, monopolies, even churches were targets for its wildest attacks. The *Journal,* and even the more responsible *World,* rode the crest of popular sentiments and issues and even created them. Exaggerated reports, for example of poor social conditions in Cuba, were daily breakfast fare for millions of *Journal* and *World* readers. Witness this exchange of cables between an illustrator for the *Journal* and William Randolph Hearst:

(TO) HEARST, JOURNAL, NEW YORK:
EVERYTHING IS QUIET. THERE IS NO TROUBLE HERE.
THERE WILL BE NO WAR. WISH TO RETURN. (SIGNED)
REMINGTON

(TO) REMINGTON, HAVANA, CUBA:
PLEASE REMAIN. YOU FURNISH THE PICTURES AND
I'LL FURNISH THE WAR. (SIGNED) HEARST [13]

The *Journal's* sensational reporting of conditions in Cuba, coupled with the sinking of the *Maine* in the Havana harbor, played a large part in fanning the fervor that led to the Spanish-American War.

One purpose for printing the news has traditionally been to counteract rumor. But Hearst's brand of journalism seemed to enjoy promoting rumor. If truth wouldn't sell papers, lurid detail would. So would blazing headlines and colorful comics. In fact, it was the comic strip figure of the "Yellow Kid" that gave yellow journalism its name.

In their fervent grab for news, Hearst's *Journal* and Pulitzer's *World* accused each other of stealing material. One way to test their suspicions was to plant phony items. For example, the *Journal* once planted in a list of war dead the name "Reflipe W. Thenuz." The name showed up later in the *World* and turned out to be a twisting of the words "We pilfer" (backwards) "the news"!

The *World* decided it had to get even. It hid the name "Lister A. Raah" among its listings. Duly picked up by the *Journal,* that anagram unscrambled as "Hearst à liar."

With the assassination of President William McKinley in 1901, yellow journalism lost its audience. Hearst's *Journal* had repeatedly attacked McKinley, both during and after his 1896 and 1900 campaigns. The writer Ambrose Bierce (Mark Twain and Stephen Crane also wrote for the *Journal* at one time) wrote this jingle shortly after the earlier assassination of Kentucky governor Goebel:

> *The bullet that pierced Goebel's breast*
> *Can not be found in all the West;*
> *Good reason, it is speeding here*
> *To stretch McKinley on his bier.*[14]

[13] Quoted by Mott, *American Journalism,* p. 529.

[14] Quoted by Mott, *American Journalism,* p. 541.

22

When McKinley was shot, his assassin was found to be carrying an issue of the *Journal,* one that contained an anti-McKinley editorial.

That did it. The public's conscience took over. People refused to buy the *Journal.* Clubs boycotted it and circulation fell off, never to increase significantly again.

Hearst himself lived on for half a century. He ruled a newspaper empire of thirty dailies and magazines. When Orson Welles's film *Citizen Kane* came out in 1941, people recognized it as a thinly disguised portrait of the newspaper emperor himself.

Yellow journalists had waged crusades; they'd campaigned against (or for) war, against bribery in city government, and against monopolies. For better or for worse, they had freely engaged in biased advocacy journalism. Little attempt was made to be objective.

When yellow journalism fell off and newspapers became more objective in their reporting, magazines took up the issues. (Magazines had traditionally offered points of view rather than just news.) Among the most successful were *McClure's, Cosmopolitan,* and *Collier's.* Certain editors and writers for these magazines became the muckrakers—those famous crusading ancestors of our modern investigative journalists.

Ida Tarbell was one such writer-crusader. She was also a prominent feminist of her day. From 1894 to 1906 Tarbell was an editor of the leading muckraking journal *McClure's,* which published articles exposing corruption in industry and politics and also advocated the need for reform. The magazine's exposés contributed to the growing Populist movement in the 1890s, whose members supported, among other things, government ownership of railways and a graduated income tax.

In 1904 Tarbell published the *History of the Standard Oil Company,* a two-volume work that cataloged the evils of the large monopoly and the cutthroat practices it used to wipe out the competition. As a result of this exposé, President William Howard Taft invoked the Sherman Anti-Trust Act in 1911 and dissolved the Standard Oil trust.

Tarbell left *McClure's* not long after publication of her book to form *American Magazine* with, among others, William Allen White of *Emporia* (Kansas) *Gazette* fame and the leading muckraker, Lincoln Steffens. *The Shame of the Cities* (1904) was a collection of Steffens's muckraking articles from *McClure's*.

In *Collier's* magazine, Samuel Hopkins Adams published an exposé of the patent medicine trade. His article, called "The Great American Fraud," led to the federal Pure Food and Drug Act of 1906. Also in 1906, Upton Sinclair published the famous muckraking novel *The Jungle,* detailing the working lives of immigrants in Chicago's stockyards and exposing the unhealthy conditions of the meat-packing industry there. As a result of the aroused sentiment, that same year Congress passed the Meat Inspection Act, which became a milestone in consumer protection.

Theodore Roosevelt, although he encouraged responsible criticism, scorned the excesses—the overemphasis on the sordid details—of muckraking. He felt that Tarbell, Sinclair, Steffens, and the other crusaders had a fixation for "muck" (dung, manure) and likened them to the Man with the Muckrake pictured in John Bunyan's *Pilgrim's Progress,* who "could look no way but downward," even when the crown of heaven was offered him. The name stuck. But the muckrakers rather liked their label. They felt they were serving just causes, and they looked with pride on all the legislation passed because of their efforts.

Some earlier exposés had dealt with child labor. Newspaperman Jacob Riis, a Danish-born immigrant, knew firsthand about poverty on Manhattan's Lower East Side. A premuckraker, among other things he wrote about the sweatshops, which were then unregulated by law. John Spargo, a newspaper columnist and magazine writer, wrote of deprived boys in the Pennsylvania coal mines. Poet Edwin Markham wrote about an eleven-year-old girl working all night in a Pennsylvania silk mill.

Many states, even if they had a child labor law, didn't enforce it. In 1916, Congress passed the first federal child labor law. Crusading had scored again.

During the height of the muckraking era, the magazines did not let up. Crusade followed crusade. Reform followed reform. The public soon wearied, however. Though some muckrakers continued writing for a while, the movement finally came to an end around 1912. It had lasted a decade.

It would be difficult to say whether some periods do indeed generate more "muck"—corruption and social neglect—than others, or whether journalists and society are simply more on the lookout for government excesses and social ills at these times. At any rate, the muckrakers of this era brought many social ills to the attention of the public and the government. That they "could look no way but downward" profited their generation, and with child labor, consumer, and antitrust laws still on the books, we remain their beneficiaries even today.

# Chapter 3. Contemporary Investigative Journalism

Investigative journalism came into vogue, slowly, after World War II. Some early modern book-length examples are Vance Packard's *The Hidden Persuaders* (1957), about the veiled techniques of modern advertising, and Rachel Carson's *Silent Spring* (1962), which exposed the ravages of pesticides on the environment.

But our main focus must be on the late 1960s and early 1970s, for, to a large extent, investigative journalism wrote the history of those years. The reporting on the Watergate affair in the early 1970s by the two *Post* reporters, Carl Bernstein and Bob Woodward, is an example of investigative journalism at its finest and most complex. It is precisely because of its complexity and because it has been handled so thoroughly in other books (see *All the President's Men* and *The Final Days,* by Woodward and Bernstein, and *The Great Coverup,* by *Washington Post* editor Barry Sussman, among others), that we will not select it here as an example of contemporary investigative journalism. Suffice it to say that this period of acute national trauma was covered thoroughly by the press, which did its part in sharing with the public whatever information it could cull from leaks, inquiries, and interviews, so that the public could be informed about the crimes committed and about the subsequent governmental investigations of those crimes. The press in covering Watergate did its job admirably, in spite of consistent attempts on the part of the administration to cover up its illegal activities and in spite of the attempts of government investigators to keep confidential what steps were actually being taken by the FBI, federal prosecutors, the grand jury, and congressional committees to unravel the Watergate cover-up and bring the guilty to justice.

Allowing others, then, to speak for Watergate, let us take a close look at two other contemporary examples of investigative journalism, ones that also had great impact on our national consciousness. These are the publication of the Pentagon Papers in 1971 and the disclosure of the Mylai story in 1969. The first is an example of over-the-transom "leak" journalism, in which a knowledgeable party voluntarily relates or hands over confidential material or documents to the press in order to inform the public. The second is an example of an aggressive investigation by a journalist responding to a phone tip.

In June 1971 *The New York Times* began to publish a series of articles containing information culled from a Department of Defense report that had been leaked to them, called the *History of U.S. Decision-Making Process on Vietnam Policy, 1945–1967*. It was a report that Robert McNamara, then Secretary of Defense, had ordered written in the sixties, so that he and his department could understand why and how the United States had sunk into the quagmire of the Vietnam War. The motivation for the study was a creditable one—it is infrequent that a government institution has the time or inclination to examine itself, its history, or its decisions. The findings, though, became classified information, allegedly because their publication would jeopardize national security but also, no doubt, because they revealed the arbitrary, self-serving, uninformed, haphazard, or willful fashion by which government officials at times made decisions and commitments.

The *Times* pointed out the discrepancies between public statement and private deed. They compared the Pentagon Paper documents with actual records of events and found, for example, that the Johnson administration, in September 1964, was publicly saying it planned no expansion of the war while privately it was making plans to bomb North Vietnam. Other publications, such as *Newsweek* and the *Wall Street Journal,* disputed the implications raised by the *Times* and pointed to other documents to show that no contradictions really existed. Edward J. Epstein believes that the *Times* generally distorted its coverage of the subject in order to play up the duplicity theme, perhaps a justifiable motive, he says, at least historically speaking:

> *The search for duplicity in the conduct of public affairs has been a traditional and respected focus of American journalism. This is especially true in the area of foreign affairs, where it is commonly presumed that official explanations for policies are no more than convenient rationales for Realpolitik reasons of state which are never voluntarily divulged. Exposing the presumed disparity between what political leaders say in public and in private is therefore generally regarded as one of the highest forms of journalism.*[15]

The *Times* chose to print articles *based* on the study and to append documents rather than print the study itself. It was left to Beacon Press, which received its copy of the document from Senator Mike Gravel (Dem., Alaska), to publish the full and original text. Senator Gravel also entered large parts of the study into the *Congressional Record* at the time the Nixon administration and the Justice Department were at-

[15] Epstein, *Between Fact and Fiction,* p. 89.

tempting to enjoin the *Times* from further publication of the papers.

Biased or not, accounts of the Pentagon Papers were first made available to the public by the *Times*. The newspaper coverage of the Pentagon Papers thus paved the way for the public—and historians later—to gain insight into policymaking during the Vietnam War specifically and in foreign affairs in general.

Daniel Ellsberg was the inside person, the source, who had worked briefly for the Department of Defense on the study of Vietnam policymaking. It was he who had given the *Times* its xeroxed copy. In his book *Papers on the War*, Ellsberg speaks at length on his observations of the willy-nilly manner in which public policy seemed to be formulated for issues as important as the Vietnam War. He tells of the soul-searching he did before making public the information he was privy to. In discussing his final decision to tip off the press as he had the Senate Foreign Relations Committee earlier, he says:

> *Two more invasions had taken place; another million tons of bombs had fallen; nearly ten thousand more Americans had died, as well as hundreds of thousands of Indochinese. It had become painfully clear that much of Congress, too, was part of the problem; so I acted, as well, to inform the sovereign public through the "fourth branch of government," the press.*[16]

Seven thousand pages of the report went to the *Times*. The first articles appeared on June 13, 1971. "After [three] months of painstaking research, analysis and preparation," wrote Max Frankel, "the *Times* began . . . to give its readers

---

[16] Daniel Ellsberg, *Papers on the War* (New York: Simon & Schuster, 1972), p. 39.

a more orderly, though also more concise, rendering of the history than the study itself." [17]

Three days after the first articles appeared, White House lawyers obtained a court order to stop the *Times* from publishing additional articles based on the Pentagon Papers. Meanwhile the *Washington Post,* through editor Ben Bagdikian, who knew Ellsberg, had acquired a copy of the report also. At the same time that the *Times* was enjoined by the government to cease publishing its articles till a hearing could be held, the *Post* began its series of articles based on the document. Several other papers followed.

The *Post* had less than a day to organize its material. The second *Post* article was rolling off the presses when government lawyers attempted to get an injunction to restrain it, too. The injunction was denied, and the Justice Department appealed its case to the Supreme Court. Later, editor Ben Bradlee would wonder:

> [*A*]*t what exact moment did I myself confront freedom of the press as a passionate, personal, immediate reality instead of a glorious concept, lovingly taught but cherished from afar, from a seat in the audience instead of a role on this vital stage? The moment was 10:30* A.M. *Thursday morning, June 17, 1971, when silver-haired Ben Bagdikian, his shoulders bending under the burden of two heavy cartons, staggered up the stairs of my house . . . and dropped the Pentagon Papers on my living room floor. For the next 14 hours, freedom of the press, and all the legal baggage which surrounds it and tends to make it impersonal and remote, became as vivid and personal to me and my colleagues at* The Washington Post *as life itself.*[18]

[17] Quoted by Epstein, *Between Fact and Fiction,* p. 81.

[18] Quoted by Chalmers M. Roberts, *The Washington Post: The First 100 Years* (Boston: Houghton Mifflin, 1977), p. 417.

The two cases involving the *Times* and the *Post* were argued jointly before the Supreme Court on June 26. Publication of the secret report, the government argued, "could be used to the injury of the United States and to the advantage of a foreign power" and violated provisions of the Espionage Act. The *Post* argued that the Papers were historical in nature and that damage to national security was not involved. The government disagreed, insisting that the Papers did pose a grave and immediate danger, justifying the extreme and unprecedented action of imposing prior restraint, or censorship. The press countered that the government did not have the right to suspend the historic guarantee of a free press. The Supreme Court justices decided, in the end, that the government could not prove danger to national security and thereby justify its case—that of waiving the First Amendment right to a free press. The headline in the *Post* on July 1, 1971, read: "Court Rules for Newspapers, 6–3."

That the government has a right to conduct certain of its affairs in secret was not an issue in this case. What was at issue was the suspension of First Amendment rights. Restraining orders that had kept the *Times* from publishing its articles for twelve days and the *Post* for seven were lifted by the Court's decision, and soon reports again began to appear in the papers' pages. Neil Sheehan, who coauthored the *Times* articles with three other reporters, won a Pulitzer Prize that year for his work.

Daniel Ellsberg, on the other hand, for divulging classified information had to stand trial. He had gone into hiding but given himself up after only two days. Later it was learned that, in a reprisal measure, White House personnel—using CIA cameras and disguises—sponsored the break-in of the offices and files of Ellsberg's psychiatrist, to try to acquire damaging information about Ellsberg. They found nothing. The administration also, it was learned, offered the judge in the Ellsberg trial a high government post. The judge, however, politely declined and threw the Ellsberg case out of court, on the grounds that it was tainted with apparent government misconduct.

President Nixon had called the Ellsberg break-in a national security matter and requested that the Justice Department refrain from prosecuting those involved in it. But in March 1974 a Washington grand jury handed down six indictments for conspiracy to burglarize the psychiatrist's office.

When a Pulitzer was awarded that year to the *Times,* some trustees of Columbia University and others were angered. The publication of the Pentagon Papers, they said, was hardly investigative reporting since the study was an over-the-transom gift. In addition, they said, the Papers had been stolen. Others applauded the award, however, feeling that in a democracy the public had the right to know the contents of an important document concerning an unpopular war. The reporters and newspapers, they argued, had fulfilled the major function of investigative journalism—to inform the public.

Major investigative stories clustered in the late 1960s and early 1970s, a period referred to by James Dygert as "a new golden age of investigative journalism." [19] Another story with enormous impact concerned the revelations of the Mylai massacre. The reporter who investigated the incident was Seymour Hersh. (Hersh was at that time a free-lance writer, but he would later join the staff of *The New York Times.*)

On October 22, 1969, Hersh received a phone call from a young man who said the army was "court-martialing some lieutenant in secrecy at Fort Benning. He's supposed to have killed 75 Vietnamese civilians." [20] Reporters get many phone tips and are inclined to disbelieve most of them. "Catastrophe via telephone tip is a cheap commodity in Washington, D.C.," Hersh writes. But something, some instinct perhaps, made him believe this tip, and he spent the next several days telephoning friends and acquaintances all around Washington to get a lead. Some of those who knew a few details warned him not to

[19] James H. Dygert, *The Investigative Journalist: Folk Heroes of a New Era* (Englewood Cliffs, N.J.: Prentice-Hall, 1976), p. ix.

[20] Quoted by Seymour Hersh in "How I Broke the Mylai 4 Story," *Saturday Review,* July 11, 1970, p. 48. All Hersh quotes are taken from the same source.

pursue the story. "It'll hurt the army," one man said. To find out more, Hersh began "the standard newspaperman's bluffing operation, pretending to know more than I did." He was thereby able to confirm, via the telephone, that the incident in question had taken place. A call to Fort Benning advised him that an Associated Press dispatch on the Mylai incident had appeared on a back page of the September 8 issue of *The New York Times*. But details were not generally known. "Many members of Congress and many Pentagon officers knew a great deal about it. Only the public hadn't been told. But as a reporter I was still far away from being able to write about the massacre. Who was Calley? When did it happen? What happened? What were the charges?"

Another telephone call to a source gave Hersh the name of Calley's civilian lawyer, George Latimer of Salt Lake City. Latimer reluctantly agreed to be interviewed, and Hersh, on a travel grant from the Philip Stern Fund for Investigative Journalism, flew out to talk to him. After gaining the lawyer's confidence and learning the details of the case, Hersh flew down to Columbus, Georgia, and drove to Fort Benning, where Calley was supposed to be. An all-day search for Calley around the large base tested the investigative reporter's patience and wits. Hersh, strolling about with his briefcase, hoped to fool military police into thinking he was a lawyer. "Hi, I'm looking for Bill Calley," he would say confidently to the sergeants on duty. But they didn't seem to know who or where Calley was or, if they did, tried to discourage Hersh from further inquiry. "I can't tell you anything," said one captain abruptly in the Advocate General's office. A talk with Calley's military lawyer likewise proved fruitless.

Hersh next got the idea to consult old Fort Benning telephone directories. He succeeded in finding Calley's name and address but still no Calley. He then sneaked into a barracks and found a sleeping soldier who, Hersh learned, had a friend in the message center of the battalion. The friend "borrowed" Calley's personal file for Hersh's perusal. In the file was an off-base address, no help since Calley had recently moved on-base at the army's request. Reporter Hersh subsequently began going door to door in other barracks, each of which had fifty rooms. "Hey, Bill, are you in?" he'd call out casually at each door. He searched all evening without luck until finally, in a parking lot, he chanced on an officer who happened to be a friend of Calley's. The friend agreed to introduce Hersh to Calley, and Hersh managed his first interview with the twenty-six-year-old man whom the army had charged with killing Vietnamese civilians at Mylai—the figure Hersh had was 109—during a search-and-destroy mission in March 1968. Calley wanted to talk with the reporter to tell his side of the story. He confirmed many of the facts and provided Hersh with some quotes.

On the plane back to Washington, Hersh wrote his first 1,500-word article on the Mylai massacre. Though he had not been able to interest *Life* or *Look* magazines in the story, it was taken by the young representative of a small syndicate called the Dispatch News Service. Hersh also called Latimer and read the story to the lawyer—a practice usually frowned upon in journalism.

Latimer was quite pleased with Hersh's handling of the story and was able to confirm its contents later to inquiring papers. The article was purchased by thirty-six out of the fifty papers to whom it was sent by Dispatch, and on November 13, 1969, it appeared on front pages across the nation.

Over the next five months Hersh did further research and interviewed over fifty GIs who were with Calley when the Mylai massacre occurred. He wrote additional news articles and, eventually, a book on the incident.

The story opened the eyes of many Americans to perhaps the ugliest side of the Vietnam War. In 1970 Hersh received—for his stories on the American atrocities committed at Mylai—the 1970 Pulitzer Prize for International Reporting.

The Pentagon Paper articles and the Mylai stories together represent the two main types of modern investigative journalism—one an example of documents leaked to newspapers by an interested party; the other an example of a story that resulted from a tip, followed up with thorough research

34

and interviews to verify details. Both are valid types of investigative journalism.

There were many other examples of investigative journalism during this period. In December 1971 syndicated columnist Jack Anderson revealed in several articles the pro-Pakistan policy of the administration during the Indian-Pakistan war. He later released the minutes of the National Security Council meeting—which had been leaked to him—on which he had based his articles. The stories were newsworthy because the administration, including Henry Kissinger, had seemed to be neutral in its policy up to that point. Later it was discovered that the "leaker" was a navy yeoman working as a stenographer at Security Council meetings and simultaneously reporting what he transcribed to the Joint Chiefs of Staff. Edward Epstein suggests that the Joint Chiefs of Staff, in authorizing the leak of information to Anderson, may have been motivated by a desire to discredit Henry Kissinger, who was at that time making friendly gestures toward China and Russia. Thus, Epstein adds, Anderson may, after all, have been an unknowing pawn in an intragovernmental power struggle.[21] Nonetheless, for his stories on the U.S. secret pro-Pakistan policy, Anderson received a Pulitzer Prize.

In early 1972 Anderson released to the wire services a memo allegedly written by International Telephone and Telegraph lobbyist Dita Beard. This memo, supposedly intended for an ITT official, contained the information that the Justice Department would rule favorably in antitrust suits against ITT in exchange for a $400,000 ITT contribution to the upcoming 1972 Republican National Convention. Beard later testified, from a Colorado hospital bed, for a Senate Judiciary Committee hearing. The hearing lasted five weeks, but the committee found no proof of wrongdoing.

In March 1972 Anderson made still another assertion in his column—that ITT had discussed with the CIA the possibility of promoting a military coup in Chile, to prevent

21 Epstein, *Between Fact and Fiction*, pp. 13–14.

Salvador Allende from winning the upcoming 1970 Chilean presidential election. (ITT had an interest in Chilean copper mines, which had been nationalized under Allende.) U.S. interference in Latin American politics had been frowned upon ever since the Monroe Doctrine. Allende was a popular figure in Chile and considered to be—though Marxist—more democratic in his approach than the rightest politicos. Anderson's revelation confirmed what many Americans had suspected already—that government and big business had teamed up to play a part in subverting the Allende regime.

In July of 1972 *The New York Times* reported that ITT had allegedly sent to the White House a memo that discussed a strategy for toppling Allende. Later it was revealed that, in fact, the CIA had worked actively toward Allende's overthrow.

Two years of digging by Seymour Hersh, who had uncovered the Mylai story, resulted in an article in *The New York Times* on December 22, 1974, that announced CIA involvement in surveillance of American antiwar protestors during the 1960s. This surveillance included wiretapping, mail opening, electronic monitoring, and break-ins and had had President Nixon's approval for a short time. Eventually Nixon withdrew his approval, but the spying went on anyway. Hersh's investigative piece gave documentation to what many Vietnam War dissidents had already suspected.

Not all press investigations unseat a president, reveal the secret inner workings of an administration's policymaking, or uncover the tragic details of an army's needless killing of civilians. They may expose a petty local official, a police kickback, or an oral agreement by real estate agents to upgrade or downgrade a property. These "lesser" stories are really the day-to-day substance of investigative reporting. They keep municipal officials accountable to the public interest. Sometimes such stories start small but grow in significance. Watergate began as a municipal police case before it mushroomed into an issue of national concern.

Tom Gish's *Mountain Eagle,* published in the Appalachian town of Whitesburg, Kentucky, is an outstanding ex-

36

ample of good local investigative journalism. Whitesburg has only 1,800 people, yet the paper's circulation is 5,800. Gish has written stories on harassment by local police and on strip mining by coal companies. One series he did got the Tennessee Valley Authority (TVA) to open its meetings to the press. For his muckraking efforts Gish was awarded the John Peter Zenger Award in 1975 for "distinguished service in behalf of freedom of the press and the people's right to know." Muckraking is harder in a small town, asserts Gish. "A Washington editor can write anything he wants to and doesn't have to see the President. But I see the council and the merchants and the police and they see me. There's no ducking."

Business publications, too, have their Bernsteins, Woodwards, and Hershes. Reporters for *Forbes, Business Week,* and *Barron's* dig hard to unearth those activities of business and industry that might hurt the public. But the biggest business scandal of all in recent years was revealed by the *Wall Street Journal.*

It began when a disgruntled former executive of a subsidiary of the Equity Funding Corporation of America blew the whistle on a huge fraud scheme. The man, Ron Sechrist, confided to insurance analyst Raymond Dirks that his former company had sold phony insurance, altered its records, and made up fictitious policy owners. Altogether, approximately 40,000 policies were allegedly fake. As Sechrist spoke over a three-hour lunch, the Wall Street analyst scribbled notes.

Dirks, in turn, related the story to William Blundell, Los Angeles bureau chief of the *Wall Street Journal*—names, places, and whom to contact. But all the information was secondhand, so Blundell set about the painstaking job of substantiating the charges. He talked to U.S. Security and Exchange Commission (SEC) officials by phone, Equity Funding employees and executives, company auditors, and SEC commissioners. After many interviews he was confident that the story Dirks had told him was true. He gave the principals a chance to comment and then camped out in his office one whole weekend to write the story.

Blundell didn't sleep for two-and-a-half days. When the

article was completed, he sent it to the New York headquarters of the *Journal* and drove home exhausted.

"Wall Street's Watergate" shocked the entire business community. On April 5, 1973, the formerly respected Equity Funding Corporation went into bankruptcy. Blundell nearly won a Pulitzer Prize for his reporting.

Paul Brodeur is the author of a book-length exposé, *The Zapping of America: Microwaves, Their Deadly Risk and the Cover-up.* Published in 1977, the book grew out of a series of articles Brodeur had written as a staff science writer for the *New Yorker* magazine. He wrote that low frequency waves (which include radio, TV, satellites, power lines, burglar alarms, microwave ovens, CB radios, and anti-missile weapons) could cause cataracts, birth defects, and nervous disorders. He blamed the electronics industry for this microwave threat to public health. And he accused the Department of Defense for helping to cover up the danger.

Some observers believe that the kind of investigative reporting that flourished in the 1960s and 1970s has fallen off. Others say that its techniques have simply filtered down into standard reporting—that all good reporting is now investigative. Still others claim that some reporters, eager to repeat the successes of the past, look for corruption where none exists. They may lose their objectivity in the search, and sometimes their credibility.

The public's interest in long, dramatic, muckraking crusades certainly seems to have declined. Perhaps Watergate was too real and too traumatic. New Journalist Tom Wolfe called the 1970s the "me decade"—the decade in which interest in social issues declined and preoccupation with personal development mushroomed. But the less dramatic, day-to-day kind of investigative journalism persists.

The major exposés of the 1960s and 1970s had the added result of making many Americans more knowledgeable and less naive about corruption in their government. This healthy skepticism had been in short supply earlier. As Seymour Hersh wrote in his 1970 Mylai article, "Americans simply did not believe such things went on in America."

# Chapter 4.
# TV News and
# Its Investigative IQ

Television faces many of the same pressures and problems that the print media face, but on a grander scale. Controversy is somewhat less welcome in this multimillion dollar industry. Thus the investigative "IQ" of television is not as high as that of its print cousin. Network TV must generally walk a tightrope between four major groups—the advertisers, the local affiliate stations, the public, and the government. It's because of this that news divisions, under corporate pressure, must more often follow than lead. There are exceptions. But excellent examples of TV investigative reporting tend to remain rare.

Television is an expensive medium. Having no "subscribers" (public television excepted), network TV largely depends on its advertising revenue. If a program offends, the advertiser can withdraw its account. A sponsor that wants the best possible public image for its product wouldn't want that product associated with a program that offends viewers or that exposes a sponsor's wrongdoing. Equally hard to imagine on the evening news would be an investigation into the "hidden persuaders" of television advertising. It would be poor diplomacy. TV news has learned to censor itself.

Public Broadcasting Service (PBS) affiliate stations, having no ads, do not need to bow to advertisers' tastes. Rather, they survive on support from subscribers and on grants from foundations, corporations, and the government. But therein lies PBS's sensitive area. It would be unlikely for a PBS affiliate to air a news investigation of a foundation or corporation supporter. Public television must likewise be sensitive to government, from whom it receives grants. WBAI, an alternative New York FM radio station, listener-supported, is quick to point out that *it* is not at all supported by foundations, corporations, or government and so need not defer to larger interests nor restrict its programming, news or otherwise. It is, however, rare to hear conservative viewpoints or nonadvocacy programs aired on this station.

The networks—CBS, NBC, and ABC—are not only dependent on advertisers. They are also dependent on the goodwill of their local outlets, which carry their programs. If a program is likely to offend, fewer stations will carry it. Fewer stations means fewer ads and less income. Local stations are often conservative in taste. Station owners and managers, often well-off and with some status in the community, don't wish to offend local listeners, local school boards, the city council, or other civic groups. They feel they must be careful of what they broadcast. The tastes of a small community often differ sharply from those of the larger, more liberal cities, where most national programs originate.

The third group that TV networks must cater to is the public. Large networks live by the ratings. Network television is highly competitive. If a program "turns off" its viewers, viewers turn off their sets. The program can be canceled; viewers cannot be. Wheras news is a primary feature of a newspaper, it is not the main feature of television. TV news makes up only about 5 percent of a network's programming. (The rest is entertainment, though some critics also call TV news "entertainment," the reason being that so much of its content is thought, by these critics, to be mindless pap.)

The fourth and last group that networks are unwilling to offend is the government. The Federal Communications Commission was formed to regulate the broadcasting industry, first because the number of airwaves is limited and so they must belong to the public and not to individuals, and second because broadcasting has a great impact on citizens. TV is an intrusive medium. It comes right into the home. It can be turned on or off at the touch of a button. A child who cannot yet read a newspaper can work a TV switch. Parents of young children in particular are sensitive about what comes over the tube. It was due to TV's strong influence potential that the FCC adopted the regulation known as the fairness doctrine. This regulation requires television and radio stations to present, if a controversial issue is discussed, an opposing view within a reasonable time period.

Should a network or station not comply with regulations, the FCC—acting as the public's agent—can refuse to renew the broadcaster's license. (The removal of a station's license, however, tends to be more of a threat than an actuality.) Newspapers don't have big government watching them to the degree that television does. The print media don't need a license to publish; there is no agency like the FCC to take their "licenses" away. The First Amendment is their unrevokable license to publish. TV, too, has First Amendment protection, but within the FCC's circumscribed limitations.

In the 1960s and 1970s television news departments, notably CBS, tangled a number of times with the federal government. In 1971, CBS televised a documentary, "The Selling of the Pentagon." Basing his information on anonymous sources, newsman Roger Mudd reported that the Pentagon spent millions of taxpayer dollars annually wining and dining members of Congress and the business community. Why? To sell its defense program to the American public. This eye-opening report angered a number of people, among them House Commerce Committee members. When Frank Stanton, head of CBS News, refused to reveal Mudd's sources or to hand over notes and unused film clips, Stanton was cited for contempt of Congress. He appealed to local CBS stations to contact their representatives in Congress to put in a good word for him. The House ended up voting in support of Stanton.

All recent U.S. presidents have been sensitive to television and its power to portray them in a complimentary or damaging light. None was more sensitive than Richard Nixon. His administration waged a multi-pronged attack on TV news departments. Vice-President Spiro Agnew and former White House troubleshooter Charles Colson tried to pressure the networks for better coverage. Agnew's attack was especially harsh. The networks, he said, comprised a "tiny enclosed fraternity of privileged men, elected by no one, and enjoying a monopoly sanctioned and licensed by government." [22]

On October 27, 1972, CBS broadcast its first major newscast on Watergate. It was well received. A second newscast was promised for the following Monday, the 30th, but didn't appear until Tuesday, the 31st, and then in a cut, altered version. Richard Salant denied being ordered by news head Frank Stanton to cut the segment in response to a phone call from Charles Colson. But then-assistant CBS producer Stanhope Gould was later quoted in the *New Yorker* as saying that the second segment was indeed cut after a directive from top administration at CBS.[23]

CBS newsman Daniel Schorr, a persistent critic of the Nixon White House, had a particularly rough time. In a speech in 1971, Nixon promised federal aid to parochial schools. Schorr reported this but added that such aid was unconstitutional. Suddenly he learned that the FBI was investigating him. Agents were talking to his family and friends. When pressed, the White House claimed it was going to offer Schorr a government job. The job was never offered. Schorr concluded that the Nixon administration only wanted to harass and silence him—to get revenge and hurt his career.

Another time, before live TV cameras in Washington, Schorr was reading from a list Nixon aides had drawn up of the president's "top twenty enemies." The list had just been handed to him; he had no idea who was on it. He got to number seventeen and found himself reading his own name. Oppo-

---

[22] Quoted by Robert Metz, *CBS Reflections in a Bloodshot Eye* (New York: New American Library, 1976), p. 267.

[23] Metz, *CBS*, p. 269.

site his name was the tag, "a real media enemy." It was all he could do to keep a straight face before the cameras and go on reading.

In 1976, the House of Representatives came down hard on Schorr. The House Intelligence Committee had been investigating CIA misdoings. Their findings became known as the Pike Report, named for the man who headed the committee. When the report was nearly ready to be made public, it was leaked to several journalists, including Daniel Schorr. At the last minute the House, at the request of President Ford, decided to suppress the report. Most of the important items had already been made public, but not all. Suddenly alone with a now-secret report on his hands, Schorr decided that the public had a right to know its full contents.

His bosses at CBS, according to Schorr, decided the story was too hot to handle. When the *Village Voice* expressed an interest in the document Schorr decided to hand it over to them. It ran on the *Voice's* front page on February 16, 1976, under the headline: "The Report on the CIA That President Ford Doesn't Want You To Read."

No one knew at first who had leaked the story. When news got out that it was Schorr, the House Ethics Committee spent hundreds of thousands of dollars trying to find out who in the Capitol had leaked it to him. CBS put Schorr on suspension. At first, almost no one was willing to defend the newsman. Then in the following months, some press members took his side, including I. F. Stone and Carl Bernstein. Schorr appeared before the committee to testify but refused to reveal his source. The House, in the end, backed down. It voted 6–5 not to cite Schorr for contempt. Schorr, following his suspension, eventually resigned from CBS.

In April 1972 Attorney General Richard Kleindienst filed an antitrust suit against the three major networks. In 1973, Vice-President Agnew's attorneys served at least eight subpoenas on newspapers and reporters, all in an effort to find out who was responsible for the many news leaks. But one of the best proofs of intentional White House harassment appears on a White House tape in which Nixon is talking with White House lawyer John Dean and aide H. R. Haldeman:

*The main thing is the* [Washington] Post *is going to have damnable, damnable problems out of this one. They have a television station . . . and they're going to have to get it renewed.*[24]

The Corporation for Public Broadcasting and the Public Broadcasting Service were also sensitive to administration tastes. In 1973, the Network Project, the American Civil Liberties Union, and others filed a suit against CPB and PBS for censoring themselves and refusing to air certain controversial public television programs at the request of Nixon administration officials. The case was eventually settled out of court.

During the Nixon administration some observers thought that the White House was giving TV broadcasters just what they deserved. Others thought it was wrong to put pressure on any journalist in an attempt to keep him or her from exercising First Amendment rights. Certainly the administration had no legal right to wiretap the media. Officials admitted, on one occasion, that the *Washington Post* had been wiretapped. The paper spent $5,000 to try to locate the bugs, but none was ever found.

Besides needing to be responsive to advertisers, to affiliates, to the public, and to government, networks and their news departments are limited in other ways. There are certain problems, native to the medium, that make it unlikely ever to serve as a good conduit for investigative reports.

First of all, television is a visual medium. The fact that it is visual makes it highly unattractive to publicity-shy sources, though of course a TV reporter could avoid putting the source on camera. Though some sources love to be quoted in print or seen on the TV screen, others dread publicity. It has been said that if Woodward had dragged along a camera crew on his meetings with Deep Throat (the nickname of one of his primary sources), Deep Throat would have vanished and the full Watergate story would never have leaked out.

[24] Quoted by Chalmers, *The Washington Post: The First 100 Years*, p. 438.

In addition, the gathering of television news is essentially a group effort. Unlike the newspapers, it requires not a lonely reporter on a beat but a reporter plus a camera crew. The relationship between a source and a newspaper reporter is often a private one. The more people involved, the more difficult it is for the source to maintain a secret identity.

Investigative reports often deal with complicated issues. Where statistics are involved, it becomes difficult to give the statistics on television without either oversimplifying them or boring viewers with technicalities.

Further, TV is a "pretty" medium. A newsperson must have the correct clothing, a nice hairdo, good makeup. An interviewee generally may not limp or stutter—it would make the viewer uncomfortable. The emphasis on the "look" of the news detracts from the news itself. Because TV news is really more show business than journalism, its content will often be reshaped for popular consumption.

A while back WABC-TV in New York spiffed up its news program. It gave viewers a pleasant, chatty, "happy talk" news show, with smiling newscasters and humorous tidbits freely interspersed with news items—hardly the setting for sober pieces of investigative reporting. But ratings went up.

Limited air time also leads to a tendency to distort the news. News items must be cut down to a few minutes or even a few seconds. The result is often a superficial news report. There is no time to portray all the details that careful research might have uncovered—which is what investigative reporting is all about.

In addition, TV is an expensive medium. Film, cameras, lighting, studios—all cost money. It might take months to gather evidence of misconduct and put it skillfully on film. Technical problems could result in frequent delays. If a project takes too long, budget-conscious management will often simply call the whole thing off.

Sometimes, if the visual content is high, the news content will be minimal. For instance, in TV news gathering there is what is known as a "stakeout." The reporter "stakes out" the camera crew in hopes that a certain person currently in the

45

news will appear, perhaps with a long awaited statement. But that person might not wish to speak to reporters or may have nothing more important to say at the moment than "no comment." With TV lights on and cameras rolling, the tense moment is recorded on film. As a dramatic confrontation, the event might be visually exciting. As news, it amounts to very little, and its importance has been exaggerated all out of proportion. TV thus adds an element of drama not present in the event itself. The presence of a TV camera changes—becomes part of—the event.

If a reporter does a live, on-camera interview, there is no chance to verify the truth of the subject's statement with an independent source. This brings us to a major characteristic of TV news. When an event is televised, there is very little perspective, distance, or room for thought about that event. There is only what the newsperson can squeeze in, either while the event is happening or during a voice-over tacked on later. The viewer is immersed in the event itself in a you-are-there fashion. For fires, floods, riots, and battles, for presidential debates and live congressional investigations, TV news has great impact. But for less dramatic events, or the less dramatic (but just as important) aspects of those events, it is often a less effective medium than print journalism.

TV can exaggerate or distort a personality. It can make a "good" person appear better and a "mediocre" one appear worse. A fickle medium, it can make or break a person's public image.

Individuals wanting publicity or sympathy for their cause will often stage events just to gain the eye of the camera. A few start riots or threaten destruction for this purpose. Newspeople have at times unthinkingly allowed themselves to be open to such manipulation. And they admit that they have in the past been quicker to respond to rioting than to a group staging a peaceful demonstration.

Hostage takers manipulate the medium to a great degree. And the presence of TV cameras can endanger hostages' lives. When twelve Hanafi Muslims took over three buildings in Washington, D.C., in 1977, a Hanafi, spotting a camera,

46

said, "Oh, great—television. We'll hang a couple of old men out the window by their ankles. Let 'em take pictures of that!" [25] Police have advised the media to use more discretion when lives are at stake.

Finally, training for TV journalists is sometimes inadequate. Back when TV and radio were young, most reporters came over from print, where they had received, fairly consistently, solid journalistic training. This is no longer true to any great extent.

But what 'can television news do and do well? Of major importance, it can give impact, publicity, and credibility to an event in which the facts are already there. McCarthyism, the Vietnam War, the Watergate affair—TV was indispensable in bringing these events home to the American people.

Senator Joseph M. McCarthy came to wide public attention in the early 1950s when his committee hearings began to investigate large numbers of "Communist sympathizers." McCarthy kept on the hot seat all who were summoned to testify. Many people were blackballed—unable to get jobs because of their "Communist" leanings—and, as a result, several even committed suicide. Distortion of the facts, manipulation, name-calling, innuendo—nothing was beneath McCarthy in his zeal to weed out "undesirable" elements of the American population. Most people were afraid to speak out against McCarthy for fear that they, too, would be called Communist sympathizers. Finally Edward R. Murrow, a renowned CBS news reporter (remembered also for reporting the bombing of London from that city's rooftops), and his noted colleague Fred Friendly, later president of CBS News, decided to do something to stop McCarthy.

They assembled a lot of film footage. CBS, notorious for its pro-McCarthy "loyalty oath," refused to publicize the Murrow/Friendly program in advance. So the two reporters dipped into their own funds and paid for the ads themselves. In the film, McCarthy was shown to contradict himself, to

25 Quoted by John Weisman in "When Hostages' Lives Are at Stake," *TV Guide,* November 12, 1977, p. 5.

wave "proof" he never really had, to find persons guilty by association, and to use intimidation in order to obtain "confessions." Watching the cleverly spliced footage, viewers could more clearly assess McCarthy's behavior and motives—putting ideology first and people second. The two "See It Now" shows helped not only to discredit this self-appointed judge but also to mobilize those who had been afraid to speak out against him earlier.[26]

Journalists were slow in assembling the case against the Vietnam War. Public opinion against American involvement in Vietnam grew gradually in the middle 1960s. Finally, after the Tet Offensive, reports started to come in that the war wasn't going exactly the way the administration said it was. CBS newsman Walter Cronkite decided to see for himself. The result of his visit to Vietnam and of his subsequent investigative efforts was a convincing report viewed by millions of Americans.

"We have been too often disappointed by the optimism of the American leaders," said Cronkite, "both in Vietnam and Washington, to have faith any longer in the silver linings they find in the darkest clouds." [27]

As a father figure for the American people (according to a poll, 70 percent trusted him more than any other public figure), Cronkite helped sway a nation. A month after the report was presented, President Johnson, knowing the newsman's popularity and sensing a change in the tide of public opinion, halted the bombing of North Vietnam. Johnson at the same time announced that he would not seek a second term.

Watergate, too, showed the impact television could have at the right moment in history. At first people seemed to be wearying of the affair. It had been reported almost daily in the press and on evening television over many months. Then the

---

[26] In 1965 Friendly resigned from CBS in protest because the station preferred to broadcast an "I Love Lucy" rerun rather than the live Senate hearings on the growing American commitment to Vietnam.

[27] Quoted by Metz in *CBS Reflections in a Bloodshot Eye*, p. 353.

networks began televising the Senate Watergate hearings. This live testimony on nationwide TV turned public opinion around. The nation heard the confessions of cooperative-witness and White House counsel John Dean, as well as the startling revelations of aide Alexander Butterfield that Nixon had taped all Oval Office conversations. Here was live drama that the front page could never duplicate—history in the making. And the American people were eager viewers.

WNEW-TV investigative reporter Steve Bauman, working with Jack Newfield of the *Village Voice,* helped expose a big nursing home scandal in New York. Their reports paved the way for the prosecution of a major nursing home owner, Bernard Bergman, who had already been cited for many building code violations.

Another effective TV report was Geraldo Rivera's award-winning TV exposé of Willowbrook. Photographing for ABC the terrible conditions that existed at this New York State institution for the mentally retarded, Rivera woke up viewers to how their tax money was being used to provide "social services" for this segment of the handicapped.

A local station showing investigative initiative is infrequent, but in the late 1970s station KABC-TV in Los Angeles broadcast an ongoing investigation into certain unexplained shootings by the Los Angeles Police Department. Details on the shootings had been swept under the rug by the LAPD, but TV reporter Wayne Satz swept them out again. Labeled "yellow electronic journalism" by critics, the series broadcast the testimony of a source—a dissident police officer, in this case, disguised for TV behind a mask. Story followed story. Eventually the exposé picked up credibility. The *Los Angeles Times* and a city councilwoman lent their support. The series resulted in additional investigations by the District Attorney's office, the county grand jury, and other local government branches.

The ABC-TV "Close-up" documentary, "Youth Terror: The View from Behind the Gun," revealed the world of teenage delinquents. It personalized the statistics and front-page reports of violent crimes committed by youths, some reformed. It also showed what alienated young people thought and felt and how they lived. The report was a kind of *West Side Story* without the song and dance.

CBS's "60 Minutes," ABC's "20-20," and NBC's "Prime Time Saturday" are all network efforts at "magazine" journalism. These programs attempt to investigate a small number of topics in depth each week. Then there are the straight news interview shows such as "Face the Nation" (CBS), "Meet the Press" (NBC), and "Issues and Answers" (ABC). The latter are anything but slick, "happy talk" news shows. The journalist-interviewers seldom smile. Live and unrehearsed, these programs attempt serious interviewing, with tough questions (though practiced interviewees gracefully sidestep many of them), and they provide, at the least, some insight into the character of the public figure.

TV documentaries have a unique role to play. Besides "The Selling of the Pentagon," mentioned earlier, the award-winning independently produced documentaries of filmmaker Fred Weiser stand out. Up to three hours in length, his films contain no verbal commentary. Pictures and people speak for themselves. Weiser's camera is the only commentator, and its probing eye "narrates" the story. In "Welfare" and "Meat," Weiser examines two American institutions, the welfare system and the meat-packing industry. The result, in "Welfare," is an exposure of the failures of the system, which ensnares welfare workers and welfare recipients alike in the red tape of a hopeless bureaucracy; in "Meat" Weiser brings an indictment against the slaughtering industry in America for its cruel and inhumane practices.

The Oscar winning film *Network* is a brilliant denunciation of TV and its passion for ratings. In this 1976 film written by Paddy Chayefsky, a TV anchorman loses his sanity and from his crazed perspective starts to shout prophetic truths over live, coast-to-coast television. TV is not real, he says, *you're* real. Turn off your sets. Go to the window and scream, "I'm mad as hell and I'm not going to take it anymore." Though Chayefsky's film script is fiction and somewhat exaggerated, it does dramatize at least two points that this chapter

50

has been attempting to make—first that the content of television programming relies heavily on ratings (because the anchorman in *Network* is popular with TV viewers and ratings soar, he is kept on the air, even though he is obviously somewhat demented and in need of professional help) and second that the tube is subject to exploitation by causes (a terrorist group in the film is allowed TV publicity to spread its extremist views).

A panel of TV experts that included critics Jeff Greenfield and Ron Powers met on Dick Cavett's TV show one evening and sounded off about television news. They talked about the "mythology of the evening news." It's "third-class," they said, and it "ignores whole categories of news"—business news, for example. It's little more than a "headline service" that makes false claims such as "in twenty-four minutes, we give you the world." Local news programs, although "entertaining and gratifying," were also not really useful. Radio news, on the other hand, they deemed "infinitely better" than TV news.

Despite the criticism dealt it, television news is not likely, given the characteristics of the medium, to be used any more extensively in the future for investigative reports than it has been in the past. There are too many factors pulling it in opposite directions—some would say in the same conservative direction! There are too many time, space, financial, and visual limitations. And—whether TV produces or contributes to it or not—there seems to be a desire on the part of viewers to "escape" through television, to satisfy their need for light entertainment, including entertaining news. If this is true, viewers would hardly be the ones to demand better-quality, more in-depth television reporting. TV may well remain, by popular decree, what Marie Winn has called it—the plug-in drug.

Public, listener-supported, and independent television and radio stations offer some alternative to the dominant networks and often upstage them in news program quality. On PBS, the award-winning "MacNeil/Lehrer Report" frequently offers valuable in-depth reporting. It has a reputation for

51

asking hard-hitting questions of experts to gain insight into the issues of the day. Independent nonnetwork television stations make added contributions by allowing for occasional out-of-house investigative news reports. (On network TV, although entertainment shows can be produced out of house, news programs, with the exception of independent documentaries, must be produced in house. Thus, the more independent stations, it is felt, provide the viewer with a greater number of news perspectives.) Listener-supported radio stations such as KPFA in Berkeley, California, offer outlets for sometimes unpopular, sometimes one-sided or narrow viewpoints. Many of these same viewpoints, however, have been known to start with few supporters but grow into large social movements such as the antiwar movement of the 1960s.

New technologies may offer additional alternatives for the future. These include cable TV, public-access channels, and videodisks. Cable TV, with unlimited channels, has more potential for variety than do the electronic media, whose airwaves are limited. There is also the two-way cable system, developed recently, which gives the viewer an opportunity to ask questions of or to "talk back" to the system. Independent video production groups offer new, often controversial, possibilities. One of these is Image Union, which provided alternate coverage of the 1976 presidential conventions. New developments in portable videotape equipment used in a variety of different situations make unique video documentaries possible. Examples are "The Police Tapes," by Alan and Susan Raymond; "The Irish Tapes," by John Reilly and Stephan Moore; and "Chinatown," by Downtown Community TV. These, then, appear to be the newer technologies that will extend the number of news outlets and give more variety to the content and nature of TV news, including the efforts of investigative reporters.

But for now, the Cavett show experts agree that what TV does best is "visual, personalized" stories. Public TV newsman Robert MacNeil of the "MacNeil/Lehrer Report" would probably agree with them. Quoted in a New York University campus newspaper, he said:

*Television news is always going to serve a supplemental function in journalism. I don't think TV news can ever replace newspapers. It can cover headlines, personality, and debate, but it's difficult to do reasoned argument or analysis. I don't think the televised or broadcast word will replace the written word.*[28]

[28] Quoted by Jonathan L. Gitlin, "MacNeil's Views," *The Courier* 2:2, October 17, 1978.

# Chapter 5.
# Alternative Journalism

In 1976, TV newsman Daniel Schorr offered his copy of the Senate Intelligence Committee's secret report to CBS. When the television network refused it, Schorr looked around for another outlet and found the muckraking liberal weekly, the *Village Voice,* to be receptive.

In Phoenix, Arizona, Don Bolles, investigative reporter for the *Arizona Republic,* had been inquiring into organized crime and its infiltration into Arizona politics. One day he got into his car and started it. There was an explosion, and Bolles was fatally injured. Over forty of his colleagues—investigative reporters and editors from all over the country—banded together and went to Arizona to take over the work Bolles had begun and died for. Out of their five months' effort, called the Arizona Project, came a twenty-three-part series on organized and white collar crime in Arizona. Some of the larger papers disputed the reliability of the report and refused to publish it. They didn't believe in the concept of "group journalism," wouldn't print something they had no control over, or said they found the report biased. Other papers ran condensed versions, editing out some of the more controversial portions. One of the papers that published the entire report was the *Soho Weekly News* in New York, like the *Voice* a muckraking weekly. It was the only New York City paper to publish the report in its entirety.

In both of the above cases, an alternative newspaper provided an outlet by which a controversial report could reach the public.

The term "alternative press" came into use in the 1960s as referring to that part of the press concerned with alternative life-styles and viewpoints. It was counterculture (New Left antiestablishment, anti-Vietnam War) oriented and dealt in opinion as much as in objective reporting. It included straight news stories, advocacy articles, political tracts, feminist manifestos, and some investigative reports. In contrast to the commercial press, the alternative press existed—and continues to exist—basically to sell ideas rather than to make money.

The alternative press has also been called the fifth estate (an extension of Macauley's fourth estate) and the underground press. Some proponents of this type of journalism prefer the term "alternative" to "underground" because the former suggests that they serve as an option to other papers rather than as a promoter of illegal or subversive activities.

Besides providing an alternative outlet by which controversial reports can reach the public, the alternative press is important to our discussion because it is frequently the testing ground for free press and First Amendment issues—issues investigative journalists have a keen interest in. The alternative press is also, as we shall see later, the funnel through which new movements first make themselves known—often liberal or progressive movements that frequently have far-reaching effects on society.

There are those who regard with skepticism the alternative press and its contributions. Some think it has committed more blunders, page for page, than any other segment of the media. Its general lack of "establishment" respectability and sometimes offbeat content make some people uncomfortable. Sometimes they would like to suppress this motley array of papers for being un-American. Federal courts, however, have declared that the First Amendment protects all papers, not just those of the established press. Two court decisions apply here. One declares:

> *The liberty of the press is the right of the lonely pamphleteer who uses carbon paper or a mimeograph machine just as much as of the large metropolitan publisher who utilizes the latest photo composition methods.* (Branzburg *v.* Hayes, 1972)

The other decision is just as emphatic:

> *The history of this nation and particularly of the development of many of the institutions of our complex federal system of government has been repeatedly jarred and reshaped by the continuing investigation, reporting and advocacy of independent journalists unaffiliated with major institutions and often with no resources except their wit, persistence, and the crudest of mechanisms for placing words on paper.* (Quad-City Community News Service, Inc. *v.* Jebens, S.D. Iowa, 1971)

The alternative, or underground, press in America has a rather noteworthy history, beginning with the publication of a patriot press in pre-Revolutionary times, continuing with the abolitionist press in the nineteenth century and the Socialist press in the years preceding World War I, and leading up to the numerous alternative papers and magazines established in the 1950s and 1960s.

In pre-Revolutionary times, when royal governors ruled, seventeen-year-old Benjamin Franklin, alias "Silence Dogood," poked fun at the Boston establishment in his brother's paper, the *New England Courant,* an alternative paper to the governor's *Boston News-Letter.*

In the 1730s, Peter Zenger's *Weekly Journal* was the alternative paper to the *Gazette,* the official New York "court" paper. Revolutionary times saw Samuel Adams and Thomas

Paine as spokesmen for freedom in the patriot press—which began small but eventually evolved into the large, mainstream press of its day.

William Lloyd Garrison, in 1831, began publishing *The Liberator,* a voice for the then-unpopular abolitionist movement. Two years later, the American Anti-Slavery Society formed and lent the paper its support.

Meanwhile a clergyman, Elijah Parish Lovejoy, was editing the *St. Louis Observer,* a religious paper in Missouri. Lovejoy opposed slavery and voiced his opposition in the paper's editorials. Later, when he went to Illinois to edit the *Alton Observer,* he also helped to organize the Illinois Anti-Slavery Society. His efforts, however, angered many, and two of his presses were destroyed. When a gang came to wreck his newest press in 1837, Lovejoy tried to stop them and was killed.

Using Lovejoy's death as a rallying point, Northerners began taking up the abolitionist cause. The Liberty and Free Soil parties in the 1840s and the Republican party in the 1850s joined in. Finally, in 1863, Lincoln issued the Emancipation Proclamation. It was a large end for such small, "underground" beginnings. In Lovejoy's memory, Southern Illinois University now sponsors an annual Courage in Journalism award for "courageous performance of duty" in the face of community pressures.

In the 1890s, there were about nine hundred populist papers, and in 1912 several million people subscribed to Socialist papers. Before World War I, *The Masses* was the most influential underground paper. It combined Bohemianism with a muckraking Socialism highly critical of capitalist ideals. Suppressed during the war, it reappeared afterward as *The New Masses.*

Perhaps the best example thus far of responsible alternative journalism in modern times was *I. F. Stone's Weekly,* a one-man operation out of Washington, D.C., published from 1953 to 1971. In a manner untypical of most journalists, I. F. Stone avoided the use of "insiders" or sources and depended completely on his own careful scrutiny of government documents. Now a contributor to the *New York Review of Books,* Stone—investigative journalist, essayist, and political commentator—was a self-appointed watchdog over government for nineteen years. A born gadfly, he has likened himself to the prophet Jeremiah in the Bible. He believes passionately in the Constitution and the laws that derive from it. His small paper was highly critical of those politicians and departments that didn't measure up or that misused their power, and he believes that exposure is the best medicine for preventing future wrongdoing. Subscribers to Stone's weekly numbered 70,000 by the time he stopped publishing. Other publications now analyze the Washington scene, but during the 1950s and 1960s his was unique.

The *San Francisco Bay Guardian's* investigative reporting won awards for four consecutive years in the San Francisco Press Club's "Pulitzer of the West" contest. In 1969 its exposé of the San Francisco grand jury won first place. Since then, according to the *Guardian,* its muckraking has been too controversial for the Press Club awards committee to handle. In addition, says the *Guardian,* there are now members on the awards committee who represent corporations the paper has investigated.

The failure to receive recognition for its recent work hasn't prevented the *Guardian* from investigating major power centers in the Bay area—real estate interests, the Bay Area Rapid Transit, and even established papers such as the *San Francisco Chronicle* and the *San Francisco Examiner.* One exposé of the high-rise industry grew into a paperback book called *The Ultimate Highrise.* The *Chicago Journalism Review* called the *Guardian* the "conscience of journalism in the Bay Area."

*New Times,* a spin-off of *Time* magazine, for five years employed a young, forward-looking staff and featured in-depth investigative reports and New Journalism pieces. Also in the 1970s *Mother Jones,* "The Magazine for the Rest of Us," picked up the shards and splinters of the dying alternative papers of the 1960s and has enjoyed a fair following since.

This magazine, with a left-of-center tilt, generally runs articles similar to a critical piece that appeared in its December 1979 issue: "The Twisted Roots of Jonestown," which discusses the insufficient government investigations into the deaths, mostly of blacks, at Jonestown, Guyana.

The *Village Voice,* established in 1955, is considered the cream of the 1960s underground papers. As feminist writer Ellen Frankfort explains, the *Voice* was "astute at sensing the dishonesty of everyone, including the President (long before the Dan Rathers, the Walter Cronkites, even the Tom Wickers did)." [29] The *Voice* has consistently published good writers, including investigative journalist Ron Rosenbaum and advocacy journalist Jack Newfield. In 1970 it began to publish a regular column by Frankfort herself, and for her work she was honored by the Media Workshop as "the first writer to combine health issues with feminist politics." Her *Voice* investigative reports, for instance, provided the first inroads into the medical establishment's now well-documented bias against women.

For a while in limbo between being an alternative and an establishment paper, the *Village Voice* changed hands several times and was finally bought in 1976 by Australian newspaper mogul Rupert Murdoch. It is no longer considered by most to be an alternative paper.

The undergrounds [30] of the 1960s and 1970s usually had no powerful, monied interests—so they had little to lose. *The Great Speckled Bird* did hard investigative reporting in Atlanta. Houston's *Space City* raked local muck and filled the vacuum left by Houston's other papers. *Hard Times,* later absorbed by *Ramparts,* did investigative pieces. Popular with

---

29 Ellen Frankfort, *The Voice: Life at the Village Voice* (New York: Morrow, 1976), p. 7.

30 Some underground papers, taking off on *The New York Times* motto "All the news that's fit to print," told their readers that *they* published "All the news *unfit* to print"; *Rolling Stone* printed on its front page "All the News That Fits," and the *Madness Network News,* a newspaper on mental patients' rights, prints "All the fits that's news to print."

underground editors across the country, *Hard Times* had as consulting editor Ralph Nader, who also founded the consumer-oriented Center for the Study of Responsive Law. "Nader's Raiders" publish books that are a cross-fertilization of consumer advocacy and investigative reporting and his organization has itself been the subject of investigative reports.

The fifteen *major* underground papers in the Underground Press Syndicate (UPS) in 1969 had a combined circulation totaling over one million. Another figure puts it at five million in 1970. There were about three hundred papers in 1970, not including high school undergrounds. With multiple readers per copy, the underground press has been estimated as having reached 18 million readers by the early 1970s. Since then, however, the number of alternative papers has greatly decreased; only 150 newspapers and magazines that "chronicle social change" are currently listed in the Alternative Press Index.

Some of the undergrounds of the 1960s and 1970s were shoddy, unliterary products. They were at various times known as the "outlaw press," the "outhouse press," and the "seedier media." Although alternative/underground papers generally lack the "respectability" of the established press, they are important in several ways. They can print investigative stories that the established press finds too awkward to handle, such as the Pike Report (described in chapter 4) and the Arizona Project report (mentioned at the beginning of this chapter) or stories that the established press simply lacks the inclination or motivation to initiate. They also provide a continual test of the First Amendment's free press guarantee—important to investigative reporters and in fact to all journalists—in both the commercial and the alternative press. And the alternative papers nurture important social movements in their beginning, unpopular stages.

Alternative journalists were frequently harassed in the 1960s. Some underground newspaper offices were searched by police without warrants, who said they were looking for drugs. A long-haired hippie hawking a paper on a streetcorner might be arrested for loitering. When the authorities made it illegal to sell weeklies in Chicago's Loop, the American Civil Liberties Union objected. It claimed that the new law arbitrarily discriminated against the underground press.

In 1970 a printer, Bill Schanen, published several papers, including a Milwaukee underground called the *Kaleidoscope*. When his other clients found out, they canceled their ads and subscriptions. In the boycott Schanen lost $200,000. But he insisted that the *Kaleidoscope* had a right to be printed and refused to stop publishing it.

In 1969 the *San Diego Street Journal* published several investigatory reports alleging the misconduct and corruption of some leading San Diego citizens. Shortly after that, shots were fired through the newspaper office's window. Typesetting equipment was destroyed, *Journal* street vendors were arrested, and the *Journal's* car was firebombed—all with little police investigation.

In Jackson, Mississippi, the *Kudzu* survived with the help of the Lawyers Constitutional Defense Committee, an offshoot of the American Civil Liberties Union. In New Orleans the ACLU came to the aid of street vendors—harassed by police —peddling the *Nola Express,* a paper that published political exposés of the local power structure. A federal district court judge said in a hearing that evidence "overwhelmingly established a policy of the police to arrest persons selling underground papers under the guise they were impeding pedestrian traffic." [31]

Sometimes the established press has come quickly to the aid of an underground paper in distress. When police entered the offices of the *Dallas Notes,* took typewriters into "protective custody," and arrested the editor on obscenity charges, the *Wall Street Journal* was concerned enough to print the story.

Even though the established press usually doesn't want to be identified with the "seedier media," at times it feels morally obligated to speak out, knowing only too well that if free-

---

[31] Quoted by Laurence Leamer, *The Paper Revolutionaries: The Rise of the Underground Press* (New York: Simon & Schuster, 1972), p. 148.

dom of the press ends for underground papers, it ends for all papers.

However, there are other times when the established press has been slow to step in to defend the underground press. The *Los Angeles Free Press* (*"Freep"*), in a controversial article in 1969, divulged the names, addresses, and telephone numbers of eighty narcotics agents. The paper said its purpose was to curb the abuses committed by narcotics officers. (The information had been given to the paper by a clerk employed in the state attorney general's office.) The result was a historic case in which the state filed a $10 million civil lawsuit against both the publisher and the reporter for obstruction of justice and a criminal lawsuit for receiving stolen property. A $15 million class action suit was also filed on behalf of the narcotics agents, who charged invasion of privacy. In the first case, the lower court found the *Freep* guilty, though the judge drastically reduced the sentences given. The conviction was finally overturned by the California Supreme Court on the basis that the paper had no reason to know that the list was stolen. The other two cases were settled out of court. The publisher ended up paying $43,000 and the paper itself, $10,000. Belatedly, the *Los Angeles Times* supported the *Freep* in a September 20, 1970, editorial. It wrote: "Should this case stand and become a precedent, the impact on the investigative efforts of the press to disclose wrongdoing in government could be devastating."

Women and minorities, including blacks and Chicanos, have all had their own papers. In 1970 the militant *Black Panther* paper reached a circulation of 85,000. Huey Newton and Bobby Seale had cofounded it, and Eldridge Cleaver edited it. The feminist paper *Majority Report* was founded in 1971 by the Women's Strike Coalition and was published throughout the 1970s by Nancy Borman.

Some underground papers were devoted exclusively to the peace movement. Often these were underground military papers. The military has traditionally been a closed society. It has its own rules and even its own court system. An army's requirement of obedience, authority, and discipline has histori-

62

cally prevented soldiers from exercising their civil liberties (free speech, free press, and lawful assembly). Military and civilian ways of thinking have always clashed; the 1960s were no exception.

As early as 1966, radical underground papers on United States bases numbered about twenty. Three years later the number rose to sixty, on and off base. There were frequent attempts to ban the papers. They consistently carried reports critical of the government and, of course, the army and the Vietnam War. One paper, *Counterpoint,* out of Fort Lewis in Seattle, exposed poor conditions in the stockade. *The Bond* in New York printed stories of arbitrary discipline and cases of racism. The papers also gave legal advice to draft resisters, provided lists of lawyers, and supplied information concerning planned antiwar demonstrations. (Over a dozen San Francisco Presidio soldiers received sentences of fourteen or more years for protesting stockade conditions. Publicity later put pressure on the army, and the soldiers' sentences were reduced.) Generally the papers were geared to educate and inform servicemen about the Peace Movement. Other military papers included the *Fatigue Press* at Ft. Hood; the *Last Harass* at Ft. Gordon; and the *Veteran's Stars and Stripes for Peace* in Chicago.

An army paper publishing today—one of the few on post to avoid censorship—is the *Fort Stewart* (Ga.) *Patriot.* The *Patriot* has run investigative reports on local black poverty, pregnant women in the army, women in combat, and conditions in the post's hospital. Major General James B. Vaught, installation commander, has never tried to censor the *Patriot.* Army spokesman Phil Nesbitt says the *Patriot* used to be the only army newspaper to truly adhere to the principles of a free press. Now several other army newspapers are following the lead.

Civil liberties in civilian life are frequently tampered with also. Nat Hentoff of the *Village Voice* called New York Telephone employee Dave Newman "a true American dissenter." Newman, a job steward in a local branch of the Communication Workers of America union, put out a short-lived paper called the *Broad Street News,* which exposed weaknesses in the union's leadership. The union took away Newman's position as job steward. Newman filed suit in a federal court to assert his free speech rights and eventually won his case.

Student papers often suffer from censorship. College officials frequently impose their own rules and regulations on the student press. One school paper, the *Daily Texan,* out of the University of Texas in Austin, was planning to run an article on natural gas regulation. But a majority of those on the supervisory Texas Board of Publications were opposed to gas regulation. The article did not run.

In 1973 Judith Nielsen, a journalism major at San Francisco State, wrote a two-part investigative report on professor-student love affairs. She based her report on a confidential questionnaire sent to professors. Those who responded to the questionnaire could remain anonymous. The number of affairs proved to be greater than had previously been thought. It was a discreet report on a controversial topic. The first part was published in the college paper *Phoenix.* The second part was quickly suppressed. Nielsen was able to sell the second part to the *San Francisco Examiner,* but they killed it also. Finally it was published by an alternative paper, the *San Francisco Sun.*

In on-campus student newspapers, the bland reporting of school events usually prevails. In the 1960s, the off-campus *Peninsula Observer* in Palo Alto was published by Stanford University graduate students. It printed articles critical of ROTC (military training on campus), of Defense Department electronics research going on at Stanford Research Institute, and of the big business connections of the university. Says John Burke writing in *Rolling Stone,* it was "one of several underground papers—the *Old Mole* in Boston and the *Rag* in Austin, Texas, also come to mind—that gave first-rate coverage of their community and often developed stories of national interest." [32]

[32] John Burke, "The Underground Press," *Rolling Stone,* October 4, 1969, p. 26.

High school student reporters have been referred to as "captive voices." A high school student in Washington State, John Freeberg, was an honor student in the late 1960s and a regional winner in the competition, "What Democracy Means to Me," sponsored by the Veterans of Foreign Wars. Because he also put out a mimeographed antiwar paper, he was suspended before graduation. The American Civil Liberties Union filed suit on his behalf and won its case.

Student censorship was one of the issues taken up by the Commission of Inquiry into High School Journalism,[33] whose findings were published in a report entitled *Captive Voices*. This report, while encouraging responsible, honest high school journalism, also criticizes censorship on the part of teachers and administrators and quotes a Supreme Court decision to back up its viewpoint:

> *Students in school as well as out of school are persons under our Constitution. . . . In our system, students . . . may not be confined to the expression of those sentiments that are officially approved. In the absence of a specific showing of constitutionally valid reasons to regulate their speech, students are entitled to freedom of expression of their views.* (Tinker *v*. Des Moines Independent School District, 1969)

The decision applied specifically to students wearing black arm bands to protest the Vietnam War, but it can apply equally to all forms of free expression, including student publications—both official and underground. What *can* be censored is material that is obscene or libelous or that threatens the "physical disruption" of the school.

The commission report concluded that the First Amendment guarantees students "the right to report on and editorialize about controversial topics and events in the school,

[33] Two members of the commission are known to television viewers—Charlayne Hunter-Gault of public television's "MacNeil/Lehrer Report" and Sander Vanocur, a former WNBC journalist.

65

community, nation, and world." (Yet a survey recently reported in *The New York Times* showed that censorship in schools rose from 20 percent in 1965 to 30 percent in 1978. Materials censored included books and school newspapers.)

Also prohibited by the First Amendment is prior restraint. Yet the submission of articles to the principal for prior approval has been allowed by some courts and opposed by others. The commission recommends that school officials not demand to review articles before publication. And, it suggests, even if they do, officials may still not withhold their approval unless the articles are "libelous, obscene, or capable of creating substantial and material disruption of the school."

In Troy, New York, high school students were suspended for criticizing school officials. The New York State Commissioner of Education Ewald Nyquist reversed the suspension and wrote:

> *The student press can be a valuable learning device and an important educational resource. Its effectiveness, however, would be substantially impaired if student editors were forced to function under imminent fear of discipline for errors in judgment. The right of freedom of expression carries with it the right to make mistakes on occasion. This, too, is an essential portion of the learning process.*[34]

Young reporters, like veteran journalists, ought to be held responsible for the factual content of what they write. They should be objective and honest in their journalistic investigations and present fair and balanced accounts of their findings. But they should also be encouraged to "inquire about and report on all issues confronting them as students and citizens," says the Commission of Inquiry. "It is the Commission's hope that school officials will support the First Amendment rights

[34] Quoted in *Captive Voices: The Report of the Commission of Inquiry into High School Journalism*. Convened by the Robert F. Kennedy Memorial; prepared by Jack Nelson (New York: Schocken Books, 1974), p. 158.

of students and in so doing respect and promote the rule of law in this country's schools."

Adds *New York Times* associate editor Tom Wicker, who contributed a statement to the commission's report:

> *So, fellow journalists, the next time your local principal cracks down on a kid editor who shows some gumption, send not to know for whom the bell tolls; it's not much of a jump from there to an injunction against the Pentagon Papers.*[35]

[35] Ibid., p.136.

# Chapter 6.
# Investigating
# the Investigators

"Lie, cheat, and steal!" a reporter advises his adult education class at a large New York City university. To encourage his budding writers, he adds, "Everyone does it!"

Although the reporter teaches general nonfiction writing, some might say his words aptly describe the techniques of investigative reporting. *Lie* to get past the secretary to talk to the person who has the information you need. *Cheat* by searching a politician's desk after hours or by giving a phony name on the telephone. *Steal* secret government documents—or have an insider steal them for you—and print them in your column.

Is this really the code that investigative journalists live by? And if so, is it moral, ethical, or even legal to lie, cheat, or steal to "get the story"? Is it perfectly all right for reporters to bring judgment on others by breaking the law themselves?

These are tough questions, and ones for which there are really no black and white answers. Yes, investigative reporters do occasionally use unethical and even illegal methods to obtain the facts. But it would be difficult to say that they are always wrong in doing so.

As there are checks and balances for the three branches of government, so there are checks and balances for the press. These include the traditional thou-shalt-nots of the profession (for example, indulging in subjectivity and conflict of interest); constitutional amendments that guarantee citizens the rights to privacy, due process, and a fair trial; and laws such as the Espionage Act that aim to protect national security.

Bernstein and Woodward approached members of the Nixon Committee for the Re-Election of the President (CRP) and tricked them by saying that other committee members suggested that they might want to talk. Believing the lie, the persons approached did talk, revealing things the reporters might not otherwise have learned.

The mother of mass killer Richard Speck talked too. The man on the other end of the telephone was allegedly her son's lawyer, or so he *said*. Actually, Mrs. Speck was spilling her story unknowingly to Harry Romanoff of the old *Chicago Daily American*. That kind of trickery sells papers—and sometimes breaks laws.

Department of Defense consultant Daniel Ellsberg "borrowed" a copy of the highly sensitive Pentagon Papers and turned it over to *The New York Times* for publication. Stealing, or unlawfully receiving classified government documents, violates the Espionage Act and is said to threaten national security. But in this case the Supreme Court said the government had to show, not just claim, danger to national security if there was to be prior restraint. Since it did not, no injunction could be issued, and the Court ruled in favor of the *Times* and the *Washington Post*. (See chapter 3 for details.)

A strong case for prior restraint was made with regard to the article "How a Hydrogen Bomb Works," written by Howard Morland. The *Progressive* magazine was enjoined from publishing the article early in 1979 on the grounds that it would endanger national security, even though the information had allegedly been assembled from previously published sources and was, consequently, already in the public domain. This case resulted in the first court battle over prior restraint since the Pentagon Papers. But in the fall of 1979 a letter written by Charles Hansen (a collector of documents on nuclear weaponry) that contained a diagram of a cross section of a hydrogen bomb appeared in the *Madison Press Connection,* and the Justice Department announced it would abandon efforts to prevent the publication of the article in the *Progressive.*

This case is the peacetime equivalent to the *Chicago Tribune* case in World War II, when the paper published a story that the Allies had broken the Japanese Code. Of course when the enemy read it, they simply changed the code and the war effort suffered. It could be argued that, in this case at least, the paper should have been restrained.

Lying, playing tricks, cheating, stealing, or just plain nosing around—such behavior on the part of some journalists makes many citizens cringe. It angers them, and they close their doors to reporters—quite literally in the case of "closed-door" or "executive" sessions. It causes legislators to pass anti-disclosure laws. It causes private individuals to strike back with multimillion-dollar lawsuits. It encourages judges to issue gag orders (the censoring of the media in its news coverage of court proceedings). Judges have been known to subpoena the notes of reporters and the names of news sources and threaten reporters with jail or fines if they refuse to cooperate or if such noncompliance hampers grand jury or trial proceedings, state shield laws notwithstanding. Questionable journalistic behavior causes some people—desperate ones—to threaten reporters with bodily harm and, in some instances, to act on their threats.

A particularly humorous, if bizarre, example of "gagging" took place in the Michigan State Senate in the early 1970s. Maybe the politicians there figured that reporters in glass houses couldn't throw stones or cast aspersions. In any event the senators began construction on a glass booth to house reporters in so they could control what the "pack" could and couldn't hear and, thus, what the public could know. This was not quite the open society, with its free flow of information, that the writers of the Constitution envisioned when they provided in the First Amendment for a free press.

Another tactic that officials use is the "executive session."

70

Here they discuss public policies in meetings closed to reporters and the public alike. Of course such secret sessions immediately arouse suspicion. What, reporters wonder, are officials discussing that the public can't know about? Are officials taking advantage of their power? Are they privy to information that everyone should know and not just a few? Journalists—in their eagerness to inform the public—at times manage to crash these sessions. In addition, some states have passed open meeting laws to prevent secret sessions. Many of these "sunshine laws" were passed after the Watergate scandal. The federal government, too, with its "Government in the Sunshine" Act of 1976, passed its own law, thereby opening the meetings of many of its agencies to the public.

Another way to check the power of the press is to expose investigative reporting methods. Sometimes a reporter will quote an anonymous person with views strangely like his or her own, or invent a composite—a type or character alleged to have all the attributes of the group of people under discussion. Gail Sheehy, in her 1973 *New York* magazine investigation of prostitution, invented a typical prostitute called "Redpants," who had all the combined qualities and habits of the many prostitutes Sheehy interviewed. When Redpants turned out to be fictitious, readers were shocked. How could a reporter resort to imagination in an article alleged to be factual? Sheehy claimed that she had made it clear in her original manuscript that Redpants was fictional and suggested that it was her editors at the magazine who had passed off Redpants as real.

One could argue that making up this larger-than-life character dramatized the lives of all prostitutes and brought the truth home to the reading public. But in the traditional news story, there is hardly room for anything but pure "fact." There is more room in a weekly or monthly magazine to weave a story that tells the deeper truths that give life to otherwise dry facts. Composites, a technique in the New Journalism, have now become an accepted technique in magazine journalism. However, in the cut-and-dried news story, such techniques are still unacceptable.

There are times when reporters come under fire for con-

71

flict of interest. This will often be caught by the editors before publication or even by other reporters.

Let us say that a reporter initiates a series of investigatory articles on a candidate for public office. It is later learned that the reporter, in his or her free time, writes political speeches for the candidate's opponent. Someone can holler "Conflict of interest!" and be on target.

Two reporters did just that, in an article that ran in *Newsday* in October 1972 entitled "Newsmen Holding Paid Political Jobs, a Survey Reveals." The story was surprising—especially in a newspaper—because it is "understood" that journalists do not squeal on each other. "Some people thought it was a dirty deal for us to be going after other reporters," said Pete Bowles, coauthor of the article. Certainly, some reporters thought Bowles and coauthor Bob Wyrick were traitors. But others felt that the authors did a real service, pointing to the fact that no institution—not even the press—is free from flaw, and that the journalism profession, in this case at least, showed a capacity for self-criticism usually lacking.

Now and then reporters exaggerate facts, with or without meaning to. For this reason editors will often question reporters at length before publishing an article. They know that if a reporter is emotionally involved in a story, it is hard to stay objective and easy to jump to conclusions that the facts do not support.

Sometimes a reporter will grow to hate an official and have a secret desire to expose the person. The objective reporter controls personal bias, but if it creeps into a story the editors will make cuts, kill the story altogether, or assign a different reporter to it.

Newspaper editors themselves can be guilty of distortion —by placing a relatively unimportant story on the front page, for example, or by burying an important one on a back page. Carter administration officials who had supreme confidence in Budget Director Bert Lance were convinced of such media distortion. They claimed the Lance affair, concerning questionable banking practices, had been blown up all out of proportion because the press hadn't had a good exposé to run on the front page in a while. Lance, who was said to have written checks without the funds to cover them, pointed out that such a practice was part of accepted banking procedure. He and other administration officials claimed that the press distorted the evidence and trumpeted it in the headlines. They said that the publishing of story after story was like "prosecuting" Lance and that the "bad publicity" kept him from doing his official duties.

Even before his case could go to court, Lance resigned, insisting that he was innocent but saying that he wished to end all the discussion about him, which was putting the Carter administration, only months old, in a bad light. In April 1980 Lance was acquitted by a federal jury in Atlanta of nine counts of bank fraud. A mistrial was declared on the three remaining counts because the jury was unable to reach a verdict.

The press, in defending itself, questioned the credibility of a budget director who wrote bad checks.

Carter people considered the loss of Lance a press casualty. Once public opinion was aroused, there was little they could do to change it.

Advertisers can counter media abuse—real or imagined —especially on a local level. TV and radio are particularly vulnerable here. It doesn't have to be the loss of advertising itself. It can merely be the *threat* of that loss that makes an editor, publisher, or station owner think twice before releasing a story that could damage an advertiser's reputation. Committed to a tradition of honest reporting, the publisher might be inclined to run the story anyway. But if the advertising account is so large that its loss would threaten the very existence of the paper—which could happen in a one-industry town— the editor will probably kill the story, or at least revise it. Editors and publishers, often with the help of lawyers, have to choose between the lesser of the two evils. Sometimes their very survival is at stake. Publishing is, after all, a business.

The subpoena, a legal order directing a person either to hand something over to the court or to appear in court, has been another effective weapon against the press in recent years. In 1978, *New York Times* reporter Myron Farber, in response to a subpoena, refused to turn over his notes to the judge in a highly publicized murder trial; Farber went to jail. He and the *Times* appealed the decision, but the Supreme Court refused to rule on the case, leaving the question of source protection up to the states. This means there is still no First Amendment right to protect sources. State shield laws provide some, but not adequate, protection.

Reporters and newspaper publishers maintain that if sources must live in fear of being identified and embarrassed, then they will soon stop talking to reporters. And for the public, this means less real news.

The prospect of a long court battle, the threat of jail, lawyers' fees, and large fines have the power to weary, intimidate, or bankrupt a reporter and his or her paper, even if the case is eventually won. Subpoenas act as definite deterrents.

Lawsuits brought by private individuals, usually in the form of libel cases, also act as deterrents. Libel laws exist so that people can have constitutional protection against journalistic abuse. Libel can be defined as publishing false or defamatory statements about a person. The truth of the statements in nine states is considered in and of itself a defense. In the other forty-one states and in the federal system, the truth has to have been published for justifiable and reasonable ends. The federal basis for libel was laid out in the Supreme Court decision, *The New York Times Co.* v. *Sullivan* (1964) and is still being modified. Issues here are usually clearcut, and investigative reporters have little to fear.

But the issue of privacy is a different matter. Privacy law is growing, and privacy lawsuits flourishing, much to the dismay of the press. The notion of privacy is being tested in the courts again and again as a possible zone of safety away from a nosy press. Here is where constitutional amendments come into conflict.

Although the First Amendment guarantees free speech and a free press, the Fourth Amendment promises "the right of the people to be secure in their persons, houses, papers, and effects. . . ." U.S. Supreme Court Judge Louis Brandeis interpreted this in 1928 to mean the right to be left alone—

*from the government.* The case in which he expressed his dissenting opinion involved government wiretapping. He wrote: "To protect the right to be left alone, every unjustifiable intrusion by the government upon the *privacy* of the individual ... must be deemed a violation [of the Constitution]."

Privacy law based on *this* interpretation prevents government from meddling in our lives and in our personal decisions such as the right to marry a person of another race or even the right to have an abortion. Brandeis's opinion is often quoted.

However, privacy laws are also passed to curb press freedom and are, therefore, from a constitutional standpoint, somewhat suspect. In *Wanted! The Search for Nazis in America,* Howard Blum, a *New York Times* investigative reporter, accused a man named Tscherim Soobzokov of being a Nazi war criminal. Early in 1977 Soobzokov filed not only a $10 million lawsuit for libel but, two months later, another $10 million suit charging Blum and six others with invasion of privacy. He said that Blum in his book printed documents from Soobzokov's Social Security files. Two years earlier Soobzokov had sued CBS for $5 million on similar charges. In December 1979, the U.S. government sought to revoke Soobzokov's citizenship, charging him with concealing his membership in the Nazi Waffen SS in Germany during World War II. He came to the United States in 1955. Soobzokov denies having been a member of the SS and continues to fight deportation.

In a separate case, two *Life* reporters entered the California home of A. A. Dietemann, a suspected "quack." One reporter posed as a cancer patient. While the "doctor" waved a wand and expressed a nonsensical theory about the cause of the cancer, the other reporter secretly took pictures. A bugging device in the reporter's purse carried Dietemann's words to a car parked outside. In the car an assistant district attorney, a public health official, and a third reporter eavesdropped. Dietemann was quickly arrested for practicing medicine without a license. But later, when *Life* published an article on quackery along with Dietemann's picture, the "doctor" sued the magazine for invasion of privacy—and won. In the judge's

1971 opinion, the First Amendment did not protect investigative reporters from penalties for crimes committed while gathering the news. Dietemann recovered $1,000 in damages.

Clearly, the concept of privacy law is valid in certain circumstances. The highly respected American Civil Liberties Union supports, for example, state statutes such as the ones in New Jersey and California that permit destruction of the records of marijuana law violators. The usual intent of such statutes is to protect the reputations of young offenders innocent of really serious crimes.

But the same laws are sometimes used to prevent press investigations into suspected corruption, especially among judges and other officials in the criminal justice system. Suppose judges in a city court let certain traffic offenders—the rich or the privileged—go scot-free. If traffic records have been destroyed or sealed, how can criminal intent be proved? The *St. Louis Globe-Democrat,* in just such a case, did have access to the records and could provide evidence of traffic ticket fixing.

Judges concerned with fair trials curb the press in another way. They prohibit the media from writing about a trial before the trial takes place. Such gag orders, issued allegedly under Fifth Amendment guarantees of due process of law, have been struck down in recent years by the Supreme Court, which considers them violations of press freedom. But, to the degree that press coverage of a trial interferes with the trial itself, the courts are allowed to take action. They can prohibit the use of photographic equipment in the courtroom, move a trial to another city to avoid publicity, or hold closed hearings. In a historic decision in 1966 (*Sheppard* v. *Maxwell*), the Supreme Court acquitted the defendant because of both press and court excesses.

The free press/fair trial issue has never been conclusively resolved, though, because constitutional law is always changing and is dependent on new cases, new precedents, and new Supreme Court decisions.

Another deterrent to press power is the threat of people organizing against media conglomerates. Actually, few such monopolies exist today; the majority of newspapers and broadcasting stations are under separate and private ownership and often even compete with each other. The news media do not comprise the "block" of "effete snobs" that Vice-President Spiro Agnew envisioned. (Although the national and international news services and news syndicates do represent a kind of power block, local media still have the right to reject what they offer.)

Yet monopoly is a temptation in all big business, and in the media as well. Small independent papers fear it. And since, points out *New York Times* media reporter Deirdre Carmody, monopolies "can control a community's understanding of itself and the outside world," it is important that the public has a way to challenge them.

Generally it is felt that the media of a city should ensure a "free flow of information from as many divergent sources as possible." [36] That's what Judge David Bazelon wrote in an important decision in March 1977 for the Court of Appeals in the District of Columbia. He ruled that newspapers should not own television or radio facilities in the same town. Nor should broadcast facilities own local papers. The Supreme Court upheld his decision in November 1978. It allowed present cross-ownerships to stand but forbade them in the future. The decision was clearly a compromise between powerful media conglomerates and the public interest.

Sometimes cross-ownership, known politely as "diversification," helps keep papers alive. And where program quality is high, it can be said to provide a distinct service to the community. For example, in New York City, *The New York Times* owns WQXR-FM, one of the few radio stations in the city to provide classical music in a sea of rock.

When the public challenges the power of the media, however, reporters—traditionally "the good guys" representative of and responsible to the public interest—find themselves on the "other side."

[36] Quoted by Deirdre Carmody in "Challenging Media Monopolies," *The New York Times Magazine,* July 31, 1977, p. 24.

Court decisions, libel, privacy law, subpoenas, constitutional amendments, license renewal, editorial judgment, exposure—there are plainly many ways to oppose press excesses. No person or institution is perfect. Everyone makes mistakes, including the press. As the political pendulum swings to the right, the only danger is that, in "getting back at the press," the public endangers its own democratic need and right to know what's going on.

# Chapter 7.
# The World Press

Let us for a while leave the problems and accomplishments of the American investigative press to take a look at the world press, its problems and priorities.

It is obvious that the world press is not a homogeneous mass but a divergent mix, each nation's press reflecting the concerns of its particular people and the dominant ideology of that nation's government. It is also obvious that such a subject cannot be covered in depth in such a brief space. Yet there is no attempt here to be exhaustive but rather only to indicate, from a sampling of different regions of the world, the issues, problems, and general orientation of the press in those parts of the world. For purposes of convenience, we will group the countries of the world into three main divisions—Western, Communist, and Third World (developing) nations. The goal is one of perspective—that we might see more clearly the position of American journalists in relation to journalists in the larger world community.

Some issues to keep in mind as we go along might be the following: Is the press in a given country truly free or is it simply the publicity arm of its government? How are dissident journalists treated? Can there be a partially free press, open-minded on most issues but sensitive or downright suppressive on a few others? Are there countries where the fettered press seems to be not so much a product of the government as a product of the society? All of these issues are important and should be considered regarding the press of any nation.

There is perhaps no better place to start than Great Britain, the country from whom Americans inherited their tradition of civil liberties. Like the United States, Britain is a democratic society. But at least two factors prevail in Britain that restrict the activities of British journalists. The first is that the British are predisposed to favor a fair trial and due process over a free press. Gag orders are the rule of the day in Britain. If you publish information about a case still before the British courts, you are in contempt.

One of the most famous of such cases in recent years was the thalidomide case. Thalidomide was a drug given prior to 1962 to pregnant women and later discovered to cause birth defects. The *Sunday Times* of London, in the early 1970s, ran a series of articles on the drug. The final piece was to be about the inadequate testing of the drug by the British distributor, Distillers Company. The article never saw the light of day. The House of Lords—Britain's highest court—forbade its publication because civil suits against the distributor were still pending.

Their inability to publish the article so frustrated *Times* officials that, after meeting defeat in all the courts at home, they took their case out of Britain to the European Court of Human Rights in Strasbourg, France. The case was discussed in Strasbourg for two days in the spring of 1978, before ten judges of ten different countries. The issue was, in effect, British press freedom versus British judicial impartiality—that is, how much would relevant news stories prejudice the case in the courts?

Article 10 of the European Convention guarantees freedom of expression, but with certain limitations. In this case the *Times* was scornful of such limits. "I know of no other

80

democratic state," argued *Times* lawyer Anthony Lester, "that would suppress discussion of essential issues for ten years." [37] Thus, with profound implications for British law, the Court, in April 1978, ruled 11–9 in favor of the *Times,* and the article was published. Writes Anthony Lewis in *The New York Times* about the London *Times* thalidomide article:

> *The banning of such an article would of course be unthinkable—and unconstitutional—in the United States. Otherwise no newspaper could have investigated Watergate because a civil damage suit had been brought by the Democratic National Committee.* [38]

He was referring, of course, to the *Washington Post,* which under British law could not have published its damaging information about the Watergate conspirators because the Democratic National Committee, whose headquarters had been broken into, had filed a $1 million lawsuit against the Committee for the Re-election of the President. Because of Britain's strict contempt laws, that country could never have had a press investigation like that of Watergate.

Besides legal contempt, a second factor in British law that prevails to the dismay of many British journalists is the Official Secrets Act. Parliament can punish under its own powers of contempt those who publish "unauthorized information" —which can mean just about anything an official does not want printed. For example two British newspapers, without authorization, published prematurely a House of Commons committee report on race relations before it had been given to the full House. The newspapers were only harshly reprimanded; the penalty could have been much stiffer.

Duncan Campbell is a young British journalist who wrote for the British magazine *Time Out* and now writes for the

[37] Quoted by Anthony Lewis in "The Rights of Man," *The New York Times,* April 27, 1978, p. 23.

[38] Lewis, "The Rights of Man," p. 23.

*New Statesman.* In the past Campbell has written investigative pieces on such things as the supply of arms to South Africa, plans for the militarization of the North Sea, and the recruitment of British mercenaries. But according to the government, when he wrote about the electronic surveillance system used on American bases in Britain and pinpointed a government communications center in Cheltenham, he went too far. By receiving information from a former army intelligence corporal, John Berry, he had violated the Official Secrets Act.

The judge gave Campbell a suspended sentence of six months and "conditionally discharged" him. This meant that unless he was convicted of another offense in the next three years he would face no penalty.

A tape recording of the exchange between Campbell and the soldier was found in the home of another journalist, John Aubrey. For "aiding and abetting the receipt of information" (section 2 of the Official Secrets Act), Aubrey too was placed on probation. But both had to pay court costs totaling $15,000.

The case of the two journalists, said a spokesperson for the National Union of Journalists, will "give heart to all those who wish to create a more closed society in which journalists are unwilling or unable to expose illegal or improper activities on the part of the Government." [39] The British press organization is increasingly opposed to the Official Secrets Act, because it restricts press freedom.

A more amusing case involved a certain "Colonel B," a real person who, using this pseudonym, testified in a British courtroom hearing concerning electronics communications. The disclosure of Colonel B's real name was forbidden under the Official Secrets Act.

Finding this restriction an abuse of press freedom, three small, militant magazines promptly traced the colonel's real name and printed it. An underground campaign began to

[39] "3 Guilty in British Secrecy Trial," *The New York Times,* November 18, 1978, p. 2.

make his name famous. Subway stickers appeared. The name was even seen carved in the sand on a British beach in 10-foot letters—H. A. JOHNSTONE!

Finally Parliament got into the act. Four members of the House of Commons dared to whisper Johnstone's name on the floor. The BBC, which had just begun broadcasting sessions of the Commons, picked it up, and the colonel's name went out over the airwaves. The major newspapers printed it. When his name was at last famous all over Britain, the media went back to using "Colonel B."

The three small magazines that had first printed the officer's name were fined. The established media were not. The case so incensed British civil libertarians that they began agitating for more freedom of information and have not let up in their efforts since.

Canada has modeled its government very closely on that of Britain and has taken most of its political traditions from its former ruler. This includes its own Official Secrets Act, which, in the view of many Canadians, has put Canada, in terms of open government, light-years behind the United States. Canadian correspondents in Washington have even used the U.S. Freedom of Information Act on occasion to gain access to documents kept secret by their own government. A Freedom of Information bill was proposed in late 1979. If passed, it would help establish the right of Canadians to have access to government documents.

As a result of a newspaper's investigative reporting, the Royal Canadian Mounted Police came under fire in the fall of 1978, and the newspaper was indicted under the Official Secrets Act. The incident began when eleven Soviet diplomats were expelled from Canada for spying. Several weeks later the newspaper, the *Toronto Sun,* published a Mounted Police intelligence report on Soviet spies in Canada, a report that revealed covert and possibly illegal Canadian operations that included break-ins and buggings.

The report's publication was deemed by officials to be a breach of national security. Although another paper had also published the report, it was the *Sun,* a paper generally critical of Prime Minister Pierre Elliott Trudeau, that was prosecuted. Government harassment was alleged.

In taking issue with the indictment, the Canadian Daily Newspaper Publishers' Association called for revisions in the Official Secrets Act. Such changes, the association maintained, would make it "more in tune with the times . . . in a democratic country where freedom of the press is an essential requisite of a free people." [40]

In other Western countries the press is generally free. In France, a nation famous for its free thinkers, *Le Canard Enchaine* is an outstanding example of an investigative journal. Sweden, too, has an open system similar to that of the United States.

West Germany in 1977 put a news blackout on the kidnapping of an industrialist and the hijacking of a Lufthansa airliner to Somalia, two situations in which they felt publicity could endanger lives. Otherwise the West German press now generally values its freedom as highly as other Western democratic nations do theirs. During World War II, the Nazi party's control of the press was notorious. The title of Fritz Schmidt's postwar book, *The Press in Chains,* describes quite accurately what German newspapers suffered at the hands of the Nazis.

In Spain, which was fascist for thirty-six years, a number of press restraints were lifted after General Francisco Franco's death in 1975, and many Spanish journalists under the amnesty of August 1976 were released from prison. Though journalists in Spain have since been arrested for offenses such as insulting the armed forces, they have not been detained but were released on bail. Still, there are cases of short-term arrests and other harassments, and until the laws can be revised and consistently applied, journalists there are not completely safe. The appearance of Spanish names on Amnesty International's 1977 list of harassed journalists—the only Western European country named—attests to that fact.

Israel, a "Western" country in the Middle East, restricts

---

[40] Robert Trumbull, "Canadians Protest Prosecution of Newspaper for a Spy Report," *The New York Times,* May 1, 1978, p. 10.

its censorship to military reporting and stories about pro-Arab issues.

Western nations, with noted exceptions, are among the most advanced in the world in terms of granting freedom of the press. In Communist nations, true investigative journalism is rare.

In 1965 Vyacheslav Chornovil, a journalist from the independent-minded Soviet Republic of the Ukraine, was sent to cover the trials of a number of Ukrainian intellectuals. Chornovil came to regard the proceedings as illegal. His writings protesting the trials were published outside the USSR under the title *The Chornovil Papers*. Tried for slandering the Soviet state, Chornovil was sentenced to three years in a labor camp. After eighteen months he was released, but because he continued to write critical pieces he was again arrested and held incommunicado for thirteen months. He was finally brought to trial in 1973. To a charge of "anti-Soviet agitation and propaganda," he pleaded not guilty. His sentence was seven years' imprisonment and five years' exile.

In the West Chornovil's deeds were honored. A British newspaper prize for outstanding journalists, the Nicholas Tomalin Award, went to Chornovil in 1975 for *The Chornovil Papers*. The *Sunday Times* of London called the work "a classic product of investigative journalism."

Boris Evdokimov, another journalist from the Soviet Union, was arrested in 1971 for a series of articles he had written that were published abroad. Charged with "anti-Soviet agitation, propaganda, and links with a Russian émigré organization," he was committed to a special psychiatric hospital for "treatment."

In his book *Punitive Medicine* Alexander Podrabinek wrote about the Soviet practice of forcing Soviet dissidents to submit to such "treatment." A Russian medical assistant, Podrabinek was charged with "deliberate fabrications defaming the Soviet system," given a one-day closed trial in August 1978, and sentenced to five years' exile in Siberia.

At least twenty-four Russians, including journalist Evdokimov, are known to be held for political reasons in psychiatric hospitals. In 1977 the World Psychiatric Association, in a resolution, condemned the "systematic abuse of psychiatry for political purposes in the U.S.S.R." Peter Reddaway, coauthor of the book *Psychiatric Terror,* noted that the American Psychiatric Association was strangely silent on the Podrabinek case.

Almost from its beginnings the Soviet press has been used to propagandize and "agitate" for the collective. The press in the USSR is actually a tool of the people, the government, and the Communist party; it is not separate and independent. Topics discussed, therefore, are in most cases noncontroversial.

Craig Whitney reports that investigative journalism does exist in the Soviet Union, but it is strictly controlled and may not touch at all on certain topics. Excluded from Soviet journalistic investigation, for example, is the Soviet system itself and the policies that party leaders hand down.

Correspondents for *Pravda* ("Truth"), the newspaper of the Soviet Communist party, have a great deal of power. Authorized by the party to investigate lawbreaking, correspondents have come to have almost as much power as prosecutors, with whom they sometimes work. They might also work with the police—including the security police, the KGB. An American reporter once asked the *Pravda* chief editor whether KGB agents work undercover on the *Pravda* staff. The editor said no.

A recent trend in Soviet investigative journalism has been the exposure of waste and petty corruption. Two recent Soviet press investigations, for example, have exposed poor housing construction in western Siberia and government failure to clean up pollution in the Dnieper River.

Investigations sometimes result from letters sent by watchdog groups called "People's Control Committees." The letters appear twice a month in *Pravda* newspapers. After an investigation has been undertaken by the press, the law requires the accused to reply to the charges. In the town of Kuibyshev an auto worker observed his boss, the head of a state auto repair shop, servicing for free the cars of city officials. When the worker reported the incident, he lost his job.

The worker then wrote to a newspaper, which sent a *Pravda* correspondent to investigate. The results were an exposé that appeared on the "People's Control Page" and eventually a criminal investigation.

The press is also restricted in the People's Republic of China. Recently two editors of *Exploration,* a dissident and outspoken journal, were arrested.

In the Third World, as behind the Iron Curtain, countries prefer the press to be an arm of the government. Press activities are generally restricted, news is suppressed or censored, and outspoken editors and publishers are often harassed or punished.

In Argentina, since the State of Siege legislation was passed in November 1974, thirty-five journalists have been killed and many others detained without charge or trial. In 1977 alone, twenty journalists disappeared without a trace. Jacobo Timerman, an Argentinian publisher more than two years under house arrest, was freed in 1979 and expelled from the country. In December of that same year, a death threat against Robert Cox, editor of the *Buenos Aires Herald,* and his family was received, and they were forced to flee the country.

Gladys Diaz Armijo, a Chilean radio journalist, was arrested in 1975. She'd been writing for an underground publication following the 1973 military coup that toppled President Salvador Allende's government. After her arrest she was brutally tortured in "The Tower," an interrogation center in Chile. In 1976 she gave a secret interview about her ordeal to the *International Herald Tribune* and was put in solitary confinement for her action. She is only one of over a hundred journalists who have been imprisoned in Chile. Many others have been killed.

In 1974 seven of Peru's largest and generally conservative papers were taken over by the military government and redistributed among various sectors of the society, including peasants, factory workers, and professionals. This "socialization" of the press met with a mixed reception abroad. The *Christian Science Monitor* saw it as "another major blow at press freedom." But Zurich's *Neue Zeitung* called it a "positive step," and the Venezuelan working journalists' union said it was a "Peruvian experiment [that] holds the future of a press dedicated to the masses." [41]

The nationalized papers had previously been controlled by wealthy, conservative families—a carry-over from the nineteenth century. The present Peruvian government justified their actions by saying they found the old ownership incompatible with the new "Christian, humanist and socialist" revolution. Previously exiled journalists have been allowed to return and independent papers, originally suppressed, allowed to reopen. For a while in 1977 the latter had to submit page proofs to the Interior Ministry, but several months later restraints were lifted and the government now seems to tolerate more press criticism.

In Central America, Costa Rica has traditional press freedom. In Nicaragua, Pedro Joaquin Chammoro, editor of *La Prensa,* the only opposition paper in the country, was shot to death in January 1978. The government of President Anastasio Somoza Debayle denied any involvement.

In Africa, censorship is the rule and enforced with equal rigidity in both white- and black-controlled countries. The white South African government in 1976 arrested Peter Magubane, the internationally known black photojournalist, under the Internal Security Amendment Act. Magubane's photos on disturbances in the black township of Soweto had been published around the world, along with those of other black journalists. These photos were often the outside world's only sources of information on the racial upheavals in South Africa. Within a few weeks of Magubane's arrest, twelve other black journalists were also detained without trial. In 1977 the government closed the black mass-circulation newspaper, the *World,* and jailed its editor, Percy Qoboza, without charge. Donald Woods, the white editor of the *East London* (South Africa) *Daily Dispatch* and a critic of racial policies, was forbidden to publish anything for five years and was put under

[41] Quoted by David Dunaway and Margit Birge in "Press Experiment in Peru," *Nation,* January 17, 1976, p. 45.

house arrest. His family was persecuted. Woods eventually escaped to England.

In other African countries, journalists are liable for arrest even where there is no official government control of the media. If they choose to investigate and write on politically sensitive issues, reporters may be detained without charge as alleged threats to national security. In Uganda a number of journalists have been killed. Kenya, on the other hand, entertains the freest press in Africa and tolerates government criticism.

In Egypt, an Arab country, censorship is a fact of life for journalists. The year 1978 saw a general crackdown there on "leftist" writers and journalists. For publishing outside their country, Egyptian journalists have been investigated or censured. Said one Egyptian writer, "Sadat will tolerate pluralism, but only if it is under his control." [42] In 1980 President Sadat proposed a "law of shame" to punish those who write and speak against his policies, including against Egypt's peace treaty with Israel. The proposed law met with a public outcry from writers and other professionals.

The revolutionary Iranian government, which decried the oppressive policies of the Shah, seems no less repressive of journalists under the Ayatollah Khomeini. In January 1980, under the new regime, almost a hundred American journalists were expelled from Iran. The Revolutionary Council's action was allegedly in response to "false and distorted reports" that were sometimes picked up by the Iranian press.

Radio Afghanistan was state-run even before the Russians invaded in 1979. One of the world's poorest nations, Afghanistan began imposing Marxist policies on the backward, deeply religious Moslem nation after its 1978 military coup.

In India several hundred newspeople were jailed following the declaration of a "state of emergency" in 1975, when strict censorship regulations were imposed by Indira Gan-

[42] Quoted by Herbert Mitgang in "A Writer with Steady Work Under Sadat's Aegis," *The New York Times*, August 8, 1978.

dhi's government. The journalists were held without trial. When the opposition People's party won the general elections in 1977, it ordered the release of the political prisoners and lifted press controls. Said one Indian journalist who had been jailed, "Journalists again began writing freely—with a vengeance!"[43] It is not yet known whether Gandhi will repeat her former repressive policies now that she has once again assumed the leadership of India.

Taiwan journalist Huang Jua advocated nonviolent government reform in his native Formosa. Arrested in 1976 for allegedly planning riots to overthrow the government, he was sentenced to a ten-year term in prison. He'd served part of a similar sentence earlier. The government in Taiwan seemed to be relaxing its hold on the press early in 1979 when it allowed the publication of some opposition magazines; however in 1980 it appeared to have shifted again toward more repressive policies.

In just about every country of Asia, the government is invested with sweeping powers of arrest and imprisonment. Under the provisions of internal security legislation, journalists are often held as political prisoners for long periods without trial. Since there is no recourse in the courts, government charges are impossible to fight.

There is a general tendency in Third World nations to treat the press as a tool of the government and to charge it with the task of educating, motivating, and uplifting the masses. Peru, mentioned earlier, is a good example; its government practically forces the press to further the policies of social change and give previously excluded groups access to mass communications. The governments of Third World nations are also sensitive to criticism by the press, insisting that they are in periods of growth and require time to "get their act together." They frequently come down hard on both native and foreign journalists. Many African and Asian governments have been especially critical of Western reporters, who,

---

[43] Quoted by the Associated Press in "World's Press Enters New Year as Free as Before or a Bit Freer," *The New York Times,* January 25, 1978, p. 2.

they feel, misrepresent them by publishing their own version of the facts rather than the official government version. Western news agencies such as the Associated Press, United Press International, and Reuters, say the governments, play up the countries' revolutions and disasters and gloss over more positive achievements such as new construction and improved education.

In 1978 the United Nations Education, Scientific and Cultural Organization (UNESCO), dominated by Third World countries, proposed a code of conduct for the media— one, they said, that could govern the behavior of the world press, including newspapers, press agents, and broadcasters. The proposed UNESCO declaration met with approval from Third World and Communist nations but with opposition from the West. A compromise version was finally passed at the twentieth general UNESCO conference in Paris in the fall of 1978. This document gives lip service to the Western tradition of free flow of information but emphasizes the political need for "balance" in the news, "balance" being a Third World concept. Technically the declaration is unenforceable, but it can give certain nations, if they choose, an excuse to further censor the news and harass journalists.

A growing number of journalists around the world are being arrested, imprisoned, or tortured for merely writing, publishing, or speaking about what they believe to be true. Denied their rights, these journalists pay a high price for their personal convictions. It is precisely in closed societies where information about the government is so hard to obtain and even harder to publish that most routine journalism could be called investigative since so much information is hidden and requires a great deal of effort, patience, and courage to disclose.

In 1977 Amnesty International reported the names of 104 journalists worldwide who have disappeared, been arrested, or been detained. The twenty-five countries named included Spain and Turkey; countries of Eastern Europe; a number of nations in Latin America and Africa; plus Bangladesh, the Philippines, Indonesia, Singapore, South Korea, Taiwan, and Thailand. This listing of journalists and countries is by

91

no means complete and changes from year to year. In most countries it is difficult to obtain information on the arrest and imprisonment of journalists and writers.

Such acts are in direct violation of the United Nations Universal Declaration of Human Rights, Article 19, which asserts the right of everyone "to receive and impart information through any media" as an essential part of the right to freedom of expression. When Gladys Diaz was tortured in Chile, it was in violation of the part of the declaration that reads, "No one shall be subjected to torture or to cruel, inhuman or degrading treatment or punishment." Chornovil's rights were violated under the section that declares, "No one shall be subjected to arbitrary arrest, detention or exile."

Amnesty International is a human rights organization that works for the release worldwide of men and women imprisoned for their beliefs, color, ethnic origin, sex, language, or religion. It is independent of any government, ideology, economic interest, or religion. A consultant to the United Nations and to UNESCO, it helps to secure the acceptance of human rights by governments that routinely deny them to their citizens. In 1977 it was awarded the Nobel Prize for Peace.

In response to the growing number of journalists persecuted and imprisoned around the world, Amnesty International has set up a Journalists' Urgent Action Network. Participating individuals and groups receive information monthly on imprisoned journalists whose cases require immediate action because of torture, poor health, or threatened execution. Participants—often journalists themselves—then write letters of intervention on the prisoner's behalf to officials of the government in question. In at least fifty of these cases such messages of support have saved a life or brought about medical treatment for the prisoner. In other cases they must certainly have served to boost the morale of an otherwise lonely, forgotten, and imprisoned journalist.

Amnesty International, the United Nations, and other organizations offer some relief to the repression of journalists by acting as conduits through which world opinion can be expressed and pressure brought to bear. The Universal Declaration of Human Rights offers a set of moral principles and guidelines against which countries can measure their treatment of citizens.

Investigative reporting is not a simple undertaking even in the United States. Because of their respective Official Secrets Acts, it is a more difficult undertaking in Britain and Canada. Yet by comparison these three countries are, with respect to press freedom, among the freest in the world.

Without denying that press freedom in the United States is in constant threat of erosion due to the many conflicting interests, Americans can still consider themselves fortunate to live under a constitution that basically favors a free press and in an atmosphere in which responsible investigative journalism is respected and even depended upon to keep the democracy working.

# Chapter 8.
# Where Do We
# Go from Here?

The interest in investigative journalism in the United States seems to be declining. *New Times,* a once-successful magazine devoted to investigative reporting, folded at the end of 1978. Its death seemed to be a symptom of the age. Publisher George Hirsch said its demise was due to a lack of reader interest and to the rise of the "me decade."

*New Times* began publishing in 1973. During its five years of existence under editor Jonathan Larsen, it investigated, among other things, the dangers of using aerosol cans, certain cosmetics, microwaves, and much of the country's drinking water. It also reported the racial slurs made by former Secretary of Agriculture Earl Butz, which led to his resignation. And it published an interview with Patty Hearst's captors, the Harrises, that differed with Hearst's own defense in her bank robbery trial.

The end of *New Times* does not signal an end to investigative journalism. Lagging reader interest in political issues doesn't mean that investigative reporting stops. Reporters today still try to uncover hidden information and still get into legal battles that test laws and rulings seemingly designed to inhibit the free flow of information. If a magazine like *New Times* closes, there is still the daily press, other news magazines, and the broadcast media to carry on.

In fact, there have been some organizations formed in recent years to help make sure it does. The Reporters Committee for Freedom of the Press was established to provide free legal research and legal defense for the press and the broadcast media across the country. On its steering committee are such well-known journalists as Walter Cronkite, Barbara Walters, Tom Brokaw, and Bob Woodward. The Reporters Committee will help if a judge bans *American-Stateman* reporters from a courtroom in Austin, Texas, or if *Gazette* reporters in Charleston, West Virginia, are fined or jailed for holding back the names of sources.

The Fund for Investigative Journalism makes grants available to writers who probe abuses of authority and thus help make known the facts about hidden or complex matters affecting the public.

*New York Times* writer James Reston has proposed that the press form a Mutual Aid Defense Fund. Larger and richer papers, he says, could help out smaller and poorer ones in time of need to help meet legal defense costs.

According to Don Dwight, writing in *Editor & Publisher,* subpoenas have been handed out "like parking tickets" in recent years, at the rate of about a hundred a year. Issues *are* complex. And constitutional amendments *do* come into honest conflict. But there is a recent trend toward hindering the free flow of information, whether it is to promote the protection of privacy, to expedite due process, to ensure a fair trial, or indeed to inhibit the exposure of corruption.

Does the public have the right to know? Yes, says our government, not only is it a human right, it is a constitutional one. But it is a right subject to restriction when it interferes with other constitutional rights. At least that is the view held by the Supreme Court, the final law of the land, in recent years.

And what about the future of investigative journalism? Here in the United States, as everywhere, there are people who seek power for the sake of power—people who could topple our representative government if we are not eternally vigilant. In a real sense, the press *is* our vigilance—our eyes and our ears. Solid investigative journalism is, at least in part, what protects us from abuse, whether it is abuse by government, industry, or another sector of society. Independent and aggressive investigative reporters check and balance "the system." They keep the public informed. Like the child who sees that the emperor has no clothes, they will continue to try to tell it like it is, even though the emperor might see it—or prefer us to see it—otherwise.

# Appendix
# The Amendments

The first ten amendments to the Constitution are known as the Bill of Rights. Parts of the amendments relevant to this book are printed here.

## Amendment 1

Congress shall make no law . . . abridging the freedom of speech, or of the press. . . .

## Amendment 4

The right of the people to be secure in their persons, houses, papers, and effects, against unreasonable searches and seizures, shall not be violated, and no Warrants shall issue, but upon probable cause . . . describing the place to be searched, and the persons or things to be seized.

## Amendment 5

No person shall . . . be deprived of life, liberty, or property, without due process of law. . . .

## Amendment 6

In all criminal prosecutions, the accused shall enjoy the right to a speedy and public trial, by an impartial jury of the State and district wherein the crime shall have been committed . . . to be confronted with the witnesses against him; to have compulsory process for obtaining witnesses in his favor. . . .

# Glossary

*accountable*: responsible for conduct; used in recent years to describe the responsibility of civil servants to the public.

*adversary journalism* (also called advocacy or argumentative journalism): journalism that is highly subjective or that actively promotes a cause; muckraking; crusading journalism.

*alternative press*: the press that concerns itself with lifestyles and viewpoints different from the dominant ones; the underground press.

*antidisclosure laws*: laws that punish a person who reveals, hands over, or publishes secret government documents.

*censorship*: prior restraint; prepublication suppression or deletion of material considered objectionable; technically prohibited by the First Amendment.

*civil liberties*: freedom from arbitrary governmental interference with basic rights such as the right to free speech or a free press; freedoms protected by the Bill of Rights.

*composite*: a type or character alleged to have all the attributes of the group of people under discussion. A technique of the New Journalism of the 1970s.

*conflict of interest*: a person's competing interests; personal and professional interests that are incompatible.

*contemplative journalism*: used here to refer to essay-type journalism, written from existing knowledge without new investigation and based on speculation.

*contempt*: disregarding an order of the court or Congress; not abiding by an official order or rule.

*cover*: a counterintelligence tactic in which the covered person's mail is inspected at the post office to determine from whom he or she is receiving mail. The letters are not opened; they are merely inspected, and the return addresses are copied.

*descriptive journalism*: straight reporting of facts as seen, neither altered by subjective bias nor augmented by investigation; the conventional type of good newspaper reporting, suitable for describing almost any event.

*due process*: the course of legal proceedings dictated by law; a civil liberty guaranteed by the Fifth Amendment.

*enjoin*: to direct by authoritative order; to forbid or prohibit.

*executive session*: a closed session, one from which the public and the press are barred.

*exposé*: a disclosing of wrongdoing; a piece of investigative journalism.

*fairness doctrine*: a Federal Communications Commission regulation; demands that if a controversial issue is discussed at all on TV or radio, an opposing view must also be presented within a reasonable time period.

*fifth estate*: the alternative, or underground, media.

*fourth estate*: the press.

*Freedom of Information Act*: a U.S. law allowing anyone to examine almost all executive branch records. Passed in 1966 and amended in 1974, the law discourages secrecy in government.

*gag order*: censoring the news coverage of court proceedings by barring the news media from the courtroom, or banning trial participants from commenting on a case to the press.

*grand jury*: a jury that examines accusations against persons charged with a crime and, if the evidence warrants it,

100

makes formal charges on which the accused persons are later tried.

*indictment*: what a grand jury hands down when they find enough evidence against a suspect in a criminal case to warrant bringing the case to court.

*injunction*: a written order from the court, in which one is required to do or to refrain from doing something; the act of enjoining.

*insider*: a person who is in a position of power or who has access to confidential information; a source.

*investigative reporting*: the kind of reporting that attempts to bring hidden facts to light; objective in its approach, it aims to make public servants and others accountable for their acts.

*leak*: the act of giving out information secretly.

*libel*: defamation in print; a libelous statement can be true.

*muckraking*: advocacy journalism; slanted or biased investigative journalism; word coined by Theodore Roosevelt and used to describe early twentieth century advocacy journalism.

*off-the-record*: what a public official or other individual will say to a reporter when he or she does not wish the information given to be published; confidential.

*press*: both the print and broadcast media.

*prior restraint*: suppression or censorship of an article or other news item before publication.

*search warrant*: a legal paper granting police the right to search a premises.

*shield law*: a law that protects a reporter from disclosing a source, except in the event of a subpoena.

*source*: a person from whom a reporter receives information for a news story; often confidential.

*stenographic journalism* (also referred to here as ruminative journalism): the kind of journalism in which the reporter simply repeats what he or she has been told, without confirming or investigating the story.

*subpoena*: a legal order directing a person to hand over something to, or appear in, court or Congress.

*sunshine laws*: federal and state laws requiring government agencies to conduct meetings as openly as possible. Most of these laws were passed after Watergate, to counteract secrecy in government.

*underground press*: the alternative media.

*Woodstein*: humorous nickname given to Bob Woodward and Carl Bernstein, the team of *Washington Post* reporters who together broke the Watergate stories.

*yellow journalism*: lurid, sensational, exaggerated reporting; developed in the late nineteenth century and particularly associated with Hearst's *World*; also, the modern tabloid.

# Bibliography

*Note*: References used for more than one chapter are listed where they are of primary importance.

*Chapter 1:*
*The Gadfly That Protects Us All*

Anderson, David, and Benjaminson, Peter. *Investigative Reporting*. Bloomington, Ind.: Indiana University Press, 1976.

Bagdikian, Ben H., "Woodstein U.: Notes on the Mass Production and Questionable Education of Journalists." *Atlantic* (March 1977), pp. 80–92ff.

Dygert, James H. *The Investigative Journalist: Folk Heroes of a New Era*. Englewood Cliffs, N.J.: Prentice-Hall, 1976.

Elliott, Osborn. "From City Desk to City Hall: The Odyssey of an Erstwhile Journalist." *The New York Times Magazine* (August 28, 1977), pp. 30–36.

Epstein, Edward J. *Between Fact and Fiction: The Problem of Journalism.* New York: Random House, 1975.

"The Farber Case" (transcript). "The MacNeil/Lehrer Report" (WNET/WETA), broadcast July 28, 1978; library #740, show #4020; Robert MacNeil, executive editor; Jim Lehrer, associate editor; Howard Weinberg, producer. New York: Educational Broadcasting Corporation and GWETA, 1978.

"High Court Refuses Farber Case Review" and "The Process Due the Press." *The New York Times* (November 28, 1978).

Molotsky, Irvin. "Farber at Home, Relaxed but Angry." *The New York Daily Metro* (strike paper) (September 1, 1978).

Olsner, Lesley. "Times Reporter Jailed as Marshall Refuses to Extend Stay of Penalties." *The New York Times* (August 5, 1978).

*The Pentagon Papers,* as published by *The New York Times;* based on investigative reporting by Neil Sheehan; written by Neil Sheehan *et al.* New York: Bantam, 1971.

"The Press and the Law" (transcript). "The MacNeil/Lehrer Report" (WNET/WETA), broadcast June 26, 1978. Library #716, show #3256, Robert MacNeil, executive editor; Shirley Wershba, producer. New York: Educational Broadcasting Corporation and GWETA, 1978.

*Chapter 2:*
*A Historical Perspective*

*The Columbia Viking Desk Encyclopedia,* vols. 1 and 2. New York: Viking, 1960.

Holland, Ruth. *Mill Child: The Story of Child Labor in America.* New York: Crowell-Collier Press, 1970.

Mott, Frank Luther. *American Journalism: A History: 1690–1960.* New York: Macmillan, 1968.

Steffens, Lincoln. *Autobiography of Lincoln Steffens.* 2 vols. New York: Harcourt Brace Jovanovich, 1968.

Chapter 3:
*Contemporary Investigative Journalism*

"Boys Town Programs Plagued by Problems, Series in Paper Asserts." *The New York Times* (November 24, 1978).

Brodeur, Paul. *The Zapping of America: Microwaves, Their Deadly Risk and the Cover-Up.* New York: Norton, 1977.

Ellsberg, Daniel. *Papers on the War.* New York: Simon & Schuster, 1972.

Hersh, Seymour. "How I Broke the Mylai 4 Story." *Saturday Review* (July 11, 1970), p. 48.

Roberts, Chalmers M. *The Washington Post: The First 100 Years.* Boston: Houghton Mifflin, 1977.

"The Screaming Eagle." *Newsweek* (February 24, 1975), pp. 53–55.

Soble, Ronald L., and Dallas, Robert E. *The Impossible Dream: The Equity Funding Story: The Fraud of the Century.* New York: Putnam, 1975.

Sussman, Barry. *The Great Cover-up: Nixon and the Scandal of Watergate,* New York: New American Library, 1974.

Woodward, Bob, and Bernstein, Carl. *All the President's Men.* New York: Simon & Schuster, 1974.

Woodward, Bob, and Bernstein, Carl. *The Final Days.* New York: Simon & Schuster, 1976.


Chapter 4:
*TV News and Its Investigative IQ*

"Broadcasting Service Censorship Case to Go to Trial." *The News Media & the Law,* 2: (July 1978), p. 25.

*Bulletin.* New School. (Fall 1978).

Diamond, Edwin. "Sunday Punch." *TV Guide* (October 14, 1978), pp. 4–8.

Esterly, Glenn. "It's the Reporters Against the Cops." *TV Guide* (November 12, 1977), pp. 39ff.

Fraser, C. Gerald. "ABC Charged with Staging Gang Fight."
    *The New York Times* (August 4, 1978).

————. "17 Win duPont-Columbia Broadcast-News Awards."
    *The New York Times* (Feburary 7, 1979), sec III,
    p. 20.

Gitlin, Jonathan L. "MacNeil's Views." *The Courier* (A Voice
    for Students at NYU) 2: (October 17, 1978).

Hickey, Neil. "Is Television Doing Its Investigative Reporting
    Job?" (Part 1) and "Behind TV's Cautious Pursuit of
    Wrongdoing" (Part 2). *TV Guide* (April 2, 1978 [pp.
    2–6], and April 9, 1978 [pp. 43ff]).

Lingeman, Richard R. "Tarting Up the News." *The New York
    Times* (July 12, 1977).

Metz, Robert. *CBS Reflections in a Bloodshot Eye*. New
    York: New American Library, 1976.

Rather, Dan, with Herskowitz, Mickey. *The Camera Never
    Blinks: Adventures of a TV Journalist*. New York: Bal-
    lantine Books, 1978.

Schorr, Daniel. *Clearing the Air*. Boston: Houghton Mifflin
    Co., 1977.

Weisman, John. "When Hostages' Lives Are at Stake." *TV
    Guide* (August 26, 1978), pp. 4–9.

Winn, Marie. *The Plug-in Drug: Television, Children, and the
    Family*. New York: Viking, 1977.

*Chapter 5:*
*Alternative Journalism*

Burke, John. "The Underground Press." *Rolling Stone* (Oc-
    tober 4, 1969), pp. 11–33.

*Captive Voices: The Report of the Commission of Inquiry
    into High School Journalism*. Convened by the Robert F.
    Kennedy Memorial; prepared by Jack Nelson; distrib-
    uted by Schocken Books. New York: 1974.

Didion, Joan. "Alicia and the Underground Press." *Saturday
    Evening Post* (January 13, 1968), p. 14.

Frankfort, Ellen. *Vaginal Politics*. New York: Times Books,
    1972.

————. *The Voice: Life at The Village Voice.* New York: Morrow, 1976.

"GI's Who Question Why." *New Republic* (April 19, 1969), pp. 5–6.

Glessing, Robert J. *The Underground Press in America.* Bloomington, Ind.: Indiana University Press, 1970.

Gora, Joel M. *The Rights of Reporters: The Basic ACLU Guide to a Reporter's Rights.* An American Civil Liberties Union Handbook. New York: Avon, 1974.

Hentoff, Nat. "When the Union is Boss: Annals of Free Speech." *Village Voice* (October 9, 1978).

Kostelanetz, Richard. *The End of Intelligent Writing: Literary Politics in America.* New York: Sheed and Ward, 1974.

Leamer, Laurence. *The Paper Revolutionaries: The Rise of the Underground Press.* New York: Simon & Schuster, 1972.

Madison, Frank, SFC. " ' First to Go, Last to Know,' But not at Fort Stewart." *Editor & Publisher* (November 18, 1978).

"Mental Patients Seek 'Liberation' in Rising Challenge to Therapy." *The New York Times* (December 11, 1978), sec. I, p. 1.

Nielsen, Judith. "Lying Down on the Job at S.F. State: The *Other* Nielsen Survey." *Pacific Sun* (November 22–28, 1973).

Sim, John L. *The Grass Roots Press, America's Community Newspaper.* Ames, Ia.: Iowa State University Press, 1969.

Steiger, Richard. "The Trouble with Howard Blum's *Wanted.*" *Soho Weekly News* (May 26, 1977).

Stone, I. F. *The I. F. Stone's Weekly Reader.* Neil Middleton, ed. New York: Vintage Books, 1973.

Tallberg, Martin. *Don Bolles: An Investigation into His Murder.* New York: Popular Library, 1977.

"Teachers Find an Increase in Public School Censorship." *The New York Times* (November 25, 1978).

Witcover, J. "Media in the Mirror: A. J. Liebling Counter-Convention." *Progressive* 39 (July 1975), pp. 28–9.

*Chapter 6:*
*Investigating the Investigators*

Abrams, Floyd. "The Press, Privacy and the Constitution."
*The New York Times Magazine* (August 21, 1977),
pp. 11–13ff.
Bagdikian, Ben H. "The Little Old Daily of Dubuque." *The
New York Times Magazine* (February 3, 1974), pp. 14ff.
Blum, Howard. *Wanted: The Search for Nazis in America.*
New York: Quadrangle, 1977.
Carmody, Deirdre. "Challenging Media Monopolies." *The
New York Times Magazine* (July 31, 1977), pp. 21–24.

*Chapter 7:*
*The World Press*

"A Simple No to UNESCO." *The New York Times* (Novem-
ber 8, 1978).
Carmody, Deirdre. "UNESCO May Shelve News Code Op-
posed by West." *The New York Times* (November 15,
1978).
"Dissident Jailed." *Soho Weekly News* (August 17, 1978).
Dunaway, David, and Birge, Margit. "Press Experiment in
Peru." *Nation* (January 17, 1976), pp. 44–46.
Hale, Oron J. *The Captive Press in the Third Reich.* Princeton,
N.J.: Princeton University Press, 1964.
"Journalists and Writers in Prison" and other pamphlets. Am-
nesty International, 1977.
Lewis, Anthony. "The Rights of Man." *The New York Times*
(April 27, 1978).
Mitgang, Herbert. "A Writer with Steady Work Under Sadat's
Aegis." *The New York Times* (August 8, 1978).
Reed, Roy. "Excessive Secrecy Assailed in Britain: Some Jour-
nalists Are Objecting to Government's Traditional Re-
strictions on Information." *The New York Times* (June
4, 1978).
Schlachter, Barry. "Afghan Rulers Lean to Soviet but Act

Slowly." *New York Daily Metro* (strike paper) (September 24, 1978), p. 2.

"The Repressed Conscience." *The New York Times* (November 10, 1978).

"3 Guilty in British Secrecy Trial." *The New York Times* (November 18, 1978).

Trumbell, Robert. "Canadians Protest Prosecution of Newspaper for a Spy Report." *The New York Times* (May 1, 1978).

"UNESCO Paper on Media Reported Revised by Italy." *The New York Times* (November 10, 1978).

Van Hattem, Margaret. "Thalidomyde Injunction 'a Violation'; Human Rights Supports Sunday Times." *Financial Times* (London) (April 27, 1979).

Whitney, Craig R. "Soviet Reporters Investigate, Too, But Only Within Limits Set at Top." *The New York Times* (March 27, 1978).

"World's Press Enters New Year as Free as Before or a Bit Freer." *The New York Times* (January 25, 1978).

*Chapter 8:*
*Where Do We Go From Here?*

Carmody, Deirdre. *"New Times Magazine* Is Ending Publication: 'Me Decade' Blamed." *The New York Times* (November 16, 1978).

Dwight, Don. "Do Not Ask for Whom the Subpoena Comes, It Comes for You." *Editor & Publisher* (November 18, 1978), p. 1.

# For Further Information

The Reporters Committee for Freedom of the Press
1750 Pennsylvania Ave. NW, Room 1112,
Washington, D.C. 20006

(also publishes
*The News Media & the Law;* Jack Landau, editor)

Fund for Investigative Journalism
1346 Connecticut Ave., N.W.
Washington, D.C. 20036

American Civil Liberties Union
22 East 40th St.
New York, New York 10016

Amnesty International (USA Affiliate—AIUSA)
304 W. 58th Street
New York, New York 10017

# Index

111

112

113

115

# About the Author

Marilyn Moorcroft was born in Cedar Rapids, Iowa. She spent a year at Albert-Ludwigs-Universität in Freiburg, West Germany and received a B.A. in German from the University of Iowa. Ms. Moorcroft has worked as a copywriter, a German teacher, and a free-lance editor. She currently lives in New York City. In 1977 she published an article on the noted German writer, Günter Grass in *Commonweal* magazine. She has written paperback originals, but this is her first book for young adults.